Best Sermons
1924

Edited with Introduction and Biographical Notes by

Joseph Fort Newton
(D.D., Litt.D.)
Church of the Divine Paternity, New York
Author of "Some Living Masters of the Pulpit," "Preaching
in London," "Preaching in New York," "The
Sword of the Spirit," etc.

New York
Harcourt, Brace and Company

IN THE VESTRY

For several years past we have had each season books of the best poems, the best short stories, the best moving pictures, to which it seems worth while to add an annual book of the Best Sermons. Such a venture is not only timely, but is justified by the new interest in the issues of religious faith created by the appalling experiences of the last ten years, as well as by the debates which have recently agitated the churches; and still more by the ancient wistfulness of the human heart and its need for guidance in a time of unrest and confusion.

There are many signs to show that a reaction has set in against a too abject absorption in material concerns. Things do not satisfy; the soul has its rights and demands. Our gay and giddy-paced age, finding that the horrible gods of sport and speed and splendor have led it astray, upsetting its car of progress in a bloody ditch, is turning again to discover, as it was said of old: "The kingdom of heaven is within." To re-explore and organize the inner life, the better to fit us to cope with the bewildering issues of our age, is now a desire, a quest, and a deeply felt necessity.

In the Vestry

Where are we in religion? is a question which many who do not go to church regularly are asking in a mood of bewilderment, as if the old had become obsolete and the new not yet real. Manifestly we are in the midst of the most astonishing revolution in the inner ideal, attitude and outlook of man in respect to matters of religious faith since the days of Luther, the meaning of which we cannot yet measure. Indeed, it goes deeper than the Reformation, and its promise of liberation is more wonderful. To whom shall men turn in their perplexity and yearning if not to the man in the pulpit, and we need a book to reveal how noble modern preaching really is, when to earnestness the preacher adds insight and the art to utter those aspirations which well up in every human heart, but which so few can ever express.

Sermons come and go—they are manna for the day—but preaching goes on forever. It is a high, ineffable office, as valid to-day as at any time in the past, and its power will not die while human nature is the same. There are sermons that live for ages, made immortal by the faith of the preacher, the depth of his heart, the clarity of his vision, and the magic of his mood. Some of the homilies of Chrysostom are as fresh to-day as when they fell from his lips, and certain notes from the Middle Ages still stir us strangely. The silvery speech of Newman, ascetic and austere, devoid of pictorial illustration, with nothing but a merciless analysis of human motive and an awful unveiling of the Unseen, searches us like a flame. The golden voice of Robertson echoes in our hearts, and many of the sermons of Beecher and Brooks have in them the immortality and joy of youth.

What is the secret of great preaching? Nobody knows. It is a mystery past finding out. The wind of God blows: the sound is heard, but the source is secret. It is not in mere learning, or skill of training, or quickness of psychological perception, or splendor of oratory. No, no; the secret lies further back and deeper down. It is in the soul of the man, Spirit-born and God-illumined, his faith hammered out on the anvil of experience, his lips touched with fire by a coal from an unseen Altar. He is a man like the rest, but different: he hears "another Drummer," as Thoreau would say. St. Paul put it in one shining sentence: "Not of men, neither by man, but by Jesus Christ and God the Father."

Too often, forgetting this fact, we fear that the great succession will somehow be broken and lost— shattered by changes of thought, by the widening of horizons, by the hurried indifference of the world. Sometimes it is when the preacher loses what in radio we call "contact"; and that is tragedy. Many preachers to-day are so troubled about reconciling revelation with the shifting phases of thought that they forget the Divine message, as Christian on the Hill of Difficulty forgot his scroll. Others shrink from declaring the whole counsel of God and are shorn of power. And some, alas, infected by the nervous, jumpy mind of the time, obsessed by motors, movies, and jazz, become but one of the dramatic entertainments which the world enjoys for an hour and then forgets. Any of these is a surrender, an abdication of authority, a loss of leadership.

But true preaching is helped, not hurt, by lengthening vistas of knowledge and the setting back of the skyline. Lifting skies of outlook only make the old issues more acute and the sharp questions more poignant. The preacher must speak in the accent and idiom of his age, must know it, love it, and thrill with its passion and promise, if he is to minister to it. He must feel with the men and women to whom he speaks, must know the turns in the road and what the pilgrims carry in their packs. But he must also know that men do not go to church to hear about science, or philosophy, or even literature, much less to listen to essays on economics. They go sorely needing and sadly seeking something else. They long to hear a voice out of the heavens, some one who knows the things eye hath not seen nor ear heard. They seek, as of old, the healing touch, the forgiving word, the Hand stretched out in the darkness, which makes them know that they are not alone in their struggle for the good.

Such is the business of true preaching in every generation; and there is much more of it than we think. Many of the best sermons are neither written nor reported, and live only in the hearts of those who heard them. And not all great sermons are preached in great churches. One of the most thrilling sermons I ever heard was preached by a simple, uncultured man in a little white country meeting-house to a congregation of farmers and their families. The preacher took for his text the words of St. Paul: "Ye are God's husbandry." The trouble, he said, is that we want to be the Farmer, not the farm, to boss and not obey. He broke English grammar into forty-seven pieces, but he got his message through in a way his people saw, felt, and understood—it was tremendous! Thirty-five years have come and gone, but the sermon has been both meat and medicine to one lad who listened.

The sermons in this book, selected from a profusion of riches, show us a goodly, gracious company of preachers, very unlike one another in outlook, in method, and in gifts: young men of dawning genius, men in the full flight of mid-career, and veterans with ripe and serene vision. Hardly an echo of recent debates is heard in these pages. One would not find it easy to tell to what churches the preachers belong, if the labels were left off. They are not concerned with dogmas that divide, but with the issues and perplexities of life as men live it to-day; and above all with the problem of redemption in its tragic and gigantic modern setting. In every sermon there is the same loyalty to the personality and principles of Jesus who, in spite of all our energy and invention —radium, radio, and the rest—has in His keeping the one secret the world needs to know. About Him these preachers gather; in His name they speak, each with his own insight and eloquence, in behalf of a common faith which underlies all creeds and over-arches all sects.

The first and last sermons in this book take the same text: "In Thy light shall we see light," as if both preachers saw what all men most more and more feel, that what our tangled times need is an altogether other dimension of religion, if we are to heal the world of war and establish a kingdom of goodwill among races, classes, and sects: more Light, more Love, more Understanding—light to show us the unity of faith underlying our differing points and points of view, love to unite us in fraternity of service

and liberty of spirit, and an understanding of Jesus,
who is the Way of Love, the Truth that sets us free,
and the Life that interprets life.

JOSEPH FORT NEWTON.

Church of the Divine Paternity,
New York City.

Publisher's Note

This volume represents the church year 1923-1924: from annual conference to annual conference.

CONTENTS

Contents

THE REVEALING LIGHT

A Virginian by birth and tradition—born in Richmond in 1882, trained in Harvard University and in Union Theological Seminary in Virginia—Dr. Bowie is in the prime and flower of a remarkable career. He became a priest of the Episcopal Church in 1909, and three years later began a notable ministry in St. Paul's Church, Richmond, an adept in the difficult art of preaching to children, as well as to adults, as his books of sermons, especially *The Children's Year*, testify. During the Great War he was chaplain of Base Hospital No. 45, and after the war added to his labors the editorship of *The Southern Churchman*. In 1923 he became Rector of Grace Church, New York City, and quickly won a place of influence and leadership in the most challenging field of religious work in America. New York may be "a graveyard of preachers," but it will not inter the Rector of old Grace Church, whose genius makes him a captain of those forces fighting to stem the tide of paganism in our chief city. No one can read the sermon here given without feeling that he is a preacher of persuasive charm and power, who unites spiritual vision with grace of literary art— the personality of the prophet transfiguring the teaching of his words like the soft glow of an altar light.

THE REVEALING LIGHT

W. RUSSELL BOWIE, D.D.

GRACE EPISCOPAL CHURCH, NEW YORK

In thy light shall we see light.   Psalm 36: 9.

At the end of the published letters of Franklin K. Lane there is a fragment of a memorandum which he wrote and left unfinished on the day before his death. He has set down in that memorandum his brooding thought of what he should like to know if he passed into that other land beyond this one and could commune with the great spirits there—if, for example, he should stand in the presence of Aristotle, that mighty master of human thought. "Ah," he writes, "there would be a man to talk with! I think that I would not expect that he could tell the reason why the way began nor where it would end. That is divine business. Yet for the free-going of the mind, it would lend such impulse to see clearly."

Surely there are many who would find the echo of their own desire in words like those. "It would lend such impulse to see clearly." We grope and stumble in the shadows. A man will say of some shattering bereavement that falls upon him: "It is

3

all darkness. I cannot find any meaning in the midst of it." Or some moral perplexity involves life in its deep confusion, and one says: "I cannot see any light through all its mazes. The paths are obscure. There is nothing to show which way to go." And sometimes, not for individuals only, but for a whole civilization, the roads of to-morrow may be lost in fogs and darkness. There are bewilderments before which even the wisest grope and fumble. There is no light of clear and steady understanding by which reality might be made plain.

Light. When we use that word, we take up into our intellectual and spiritual meanings the metaphor of our physical senses. The truth and understanding which we want must have for us the values which light has as set in contrast with darkness. Let us think, then, at the beginning, specifically of what those values are.

I

In the first place, light means security, as against the darkness which is full of fear. Who is there who, at some time or other, has not passed through experiences in which the dark was crowded with its nameless terrors? Particularly in times of sickness, when the body is weak and all the tides of life are

The Revealing Light

low, there come the moments when the pressure of the darkness is appalling. Those who have been in hospitals in some long weakness, or after an operation, will remember that. Faint with the after-effects of anesthetics, or drawn down from the harborage of normal self-reliance by that strange ebb-tide of the bodily forces that sets in when the night is deepest and the morning has not yet come, the dimmed awareness of the mind floats down in helplessness as toward an ocean, vague and terrible. The horizon is filled with troubling shapes that can neither be clearly perceived nor yet escaped. The pressure of the darkness is like the pressure of heavy throttling hands. Hour by hour, the eyes may turn to the window hungry for the light, and when at last it comes, it is as though the spell were broken. The commonest sound of awaking life that breaks the dead quiet of the night is like a benediction. The light brings back the real world again, wakes into expression all its comforting and substantial friendliness, restores to eyes haunted by the phantasms of the blackness the near look of human faces, and by the flood of its brightness lifts the heart from those dark channels down which it had drifted, upon the brimming and sunlit strength of the returning tide. Neither in the darkness nor in the light is there a conscious analysis of the effect of either; but the

5

moods which they create have to do with the profoundest associations of our being.

In that terror of the dark, which in times of strength we may rise so easily above as to forget, but to which in the moments of weakness we are subjected, there climb above the threshold of the subconscious all those ancient fears that were a part of the experience of the race in those remote ages when the primitive man struggled uncertainly for the possession of his earth. Precarious battler for existence in wildernesses as yet untamed and terrible, he had good reason to dread the dark, under cover of which the great beasts prowled, and where the demons before which imagination cowered, shrieked and chattered in the winds and hid in the silence of black forests where the stillness was more horrible than sound. Grown into the deepest instincts of self-preservation was that shrinking from the dark and that looking forward to the light of morning which the long infancy of the race brought it about that men must feel. Therefore, at all times when our strength is lowered and our sufficiency is broken, the old dread of the dark comes back, and with utmost vividness of experience light becomes the token of security against fears which are the more formidable because they are nameless and obscure. When presently, then, we shall consider more specifically

6

the religious meaning of our desire for light, we shall carry into our thinking this first remembrance of what light signifies—peace, well-being, strength, as against the dread enslavements which reach hands out of the darkness to drag us down.

In the second place, out of that physical experience from which the metaphors of language come, we remember that light means not only security from surrounding dangers but definite guidance for the ends men want to reach. The traveler goes along his road. As long as the daylight lasts all is well; but the night falls, and then the landmarks disappear. The path leads into a forest and vanishes into the thick confusion of the trees, or it passes into some rocky valley, where its narrow way of safety is no longer traceable, and a man must come to a halt for fear of precipices over which a false step might carry him. The ship drives on its way under the fierce pressure of a storm. With light it could see the danger of the sea or rock or jutting coast toward which it steers; but in the darkness it is so helpless that it may point toward peril when it imagines that it is steering toward the open sea. In that vivid account of that voyage on the Mediterranean with which the Book of Acts describes the journey of Paul to Rome, it is told how they cast out the anchors and "wished for the day." Likewise many travelers before or since, not only in times of danger but in all ordinary efforts to attain their journey's end, have wished for the day. The night means confusion, and the haunted or baffled progress. Only the day can bring back the light of a guidance that is dependable.

In the third place, light is desirable because it brings back to the world both its color and its growth. Stand before any beautiful thing and watch the day decline. Look, for example, from within this Church toward any great, glowing window as the sun goes down. Little by little the colors fade. All the differentiation of its beauty sinks and blurs into a dull blackness from which all the message and meaning have gone. Stand upon a hilltop and watch the tides of daylight ebb into the west after the sinking sun and see the greenness passing from the fields, the golden glory smothered from the horizon, and all the color and variance of earth's brightness turning into somberness and dark. And then go by contrast to some mountain-top before the sun is risen. See the earth spread out below you, deep and still and yet expectant, as though touched already by the presage that quivers in the breezes of the dawn. Then see the first far pennons of the morning lift above the east. Watch the golden spearheads of the day march through the gates of the horizon and press their level

8

conquest down all roads of the retreating shadows, while after them streams the occupying splendor of the fully risen sun. See then the gray mists lift and vanish into the brightness of the sky that is turned to blue. See the green come back to the darkness of the forest, the glint to the rivers, the color to some splash of vivid flowers or to valleys with their squares of amber and green. Remember, that as the sunlight brings back to the world an infinite variety of loveliness, so from the sunlight also must all the growing things derive their power of life. If the darkness endured, they would die. It is because with every morning the light returns, pouring out its flood of energy, that leaf and stem and twig can draw their sustenance from the golden air.

Such are some of the meanings of light. It is no wonder, therefore, that, not in a shallow and vagrant way, but with a deep and cosmic consciousness, the spirit of man desires it, and desires all those spiritual realities which have for him the meaning and value of light.

Now the glory and the tragedy of life are linked together in the fact that the soul of man is forever seeking light and so often failing to find it and losing itself in the dark instead. But the beautiful promise of religion is that, through IT, light can increasingly prevail. The whole Bible is a magnificent expression of that truth. In that sublime imagination of the Book of Genesis it begins with a universe without form and void, where darkness was upon the face of the deep. Over that profound and formless emptiness brooded the Spirit of God. And His first creative word was this, "Let there be light." So the Bible begins—a void and darkness, and then a glimmer, the waking of a spark that presently should fashion, not only the universe of physical things, but the mightier miracle of man with the divine fire burning on the altar of his heart. But from the travail of that creation with the flicker of its first splendor against the mightiness of the void, the story of the Bible sweeps on until it culminates in the picture of the Holy City, bright with the splendor of a fadeless day, where the nations of them that are saved shall walk in the light of it, where the kings of the earth do bring their glory and honor into it, and where there shall be no more night.

Along the highway of human progress, which stretches from that far beginning of the world toward the consummation that is to come, moves the figure of man. For him too that road is the slow emergence out of darkness toward the light. Far yonder is Abraham lifting his face toward the stars, reflecting in that rapt look of his true glimpses of the eternal, yet involved too with the superstitions of that human childhood to which he belonged—climbing up with Isaac to the altar of sacrifice in the blind instinct that made him think that the killing of his first-born would be pleasing to God whom ignorantly he groped for, yet through the smoke of his blind and terrible devotion catching sight again of the truer light of God which he would follow. Yonder, at another journey on the road, is Jacob, that strange chaotic soul, in whom the daylight and the dark were mingled, descending now into low valleys of craftiness and deceit, and again emerging on Plains of Bethel from which to his wide eyes was revealed the ladder of God's communication, with the brightness of angels passing up and down. Farther on the road is Moses, striking the Egyptian taskmaster down in one black moment of his fury, fleeing to hide himself in the obscurity of Midian, beholding there the light of the burning bush, going back to Egypt to become the leader of his people, before whose soul henceforth the guidance of God went on as a pillar of cloud by day and a pillar of fire by night. Yonder, farther still, are the men of the time of the Judges and of the early kingdom, moving through sins that oftentimes were dark with ruthless cruelty, yet emerging into splendors of heroism like those of Gideon and Jephthah and of the great king, Saul. Behold also that most winsome figure of David, with the brightness of his gallant youth, with the high passions of his manhood covering his soul with smoke of evil through which he reached his desperate hands toward God—seeing, as a man might see the sky through broken clouds, the glory of God and the tragic shadow of his own human sin—out of the darkness crying for the light, through the night of his soul's bewilderment, climbing the mountain-tops of passionate desire and watching for the day! Nearer on the road see that other company, the greatest souls which then had trodden the highroad of the progress of mankind, prophets with their uplifted faces, Amos and Hosea, Isaiah, Micah, Jeremiah, and the others who followed in their train. *There* were men in whom the dross of the earth was being burned away in the splendor of the light of God, men who, through the often unmindful crowd of their contemporaries, into temple and common street and courts of kings alike, carried in their faces something of the high transfiguration of heaven.

Slowly, as the long road climbs height by height, the aspiring figures of the centuries move on. But still their eyes are lifted higher, and in the gaze of the mightier prophets there is reflected the triumphant wonder of that toward which they moved, and which they beheld afar. For on the crest to which the road climbs up, there on the ultimate mountain-peak of human hope and aspiration, with eyes that look down along all the infinite distance of the ascending way, and hands whose mystic power reaches out across the centuries to touch and help and lead, stands the eternal figure of Him who came out of Nazareth. "I am the light of the world," He says, "He that followeth me shall not walk in darkness, but shall have the light of life." Lifting their eyes to Him, men begin to understand the reality of what He says. There in the soul of Jesus—in the purposes which shine in Him; in the light which streams, from His Spirit and from His trust in God, upon life's perplexities; in the glory of His redeeming righteousness as it falls upon the tragedies of human sin—is the power that shall ultimately lift the shadows, make straight the path before men's feet, and pour into their hearts the strength and the desire to follow. Cried St. Paul, "God, who commanded the light to shine out of darkness, hath shined in our hearts, to give the light of the knowledge of the glory of God in the face of Jesus Christ." To the Christian mind all the course of history finds its illumination and its meaning in Him. The best that we can do, as we look to the future, is to carry forward and bring into contact with all shadowed human needs, that light of the meaning of life as revealed in Jesus. And looking backward and interpreting the progress of the human soul, we know that that which it was yearning for was that light which came reflected from the eternal conception of humanity in God which Jesus should at length incarnate. Toward the tenderness of His understanding, toward the strength of His compassionate redemption, the wistfulness of the human spirit has forever pressed forward to find that fulfilment which Jesus ultimately brought. It is as Robert Browning makes David cry in the high rhapsody with which he sought to lift the soul of Saul to God.

He who did most, shall bear most; the strongest shall stand
    the most weak.
'Tis the weakness in strength, that I cry for! my flesh, that
    I seek
In the Godhead! I seek and I find it. O Saul, it shall be
A Face like my face that receives thee; a Man like to me,
Thou shalt love and be loved by, forever: a Hand like this
    hand
Shall throw open the gates of new life to thee! See the Christ
    stand!

II

More definitely, therefore, we can now take hold of the implications of our text, "In thy light shall we see light." There is no real meaning for human life until upon it streams the light of the meaning of God. For us explicitly, as for the multitude of

14

hungry souls in their far-reaching desire, that light is best made plain in the face of Jesus Christ. When as Christians we say that He is God of gods and Light of Light, we mean that the Infinite Father whom we cannot see is like the Jesus of Nazareth whom men saw and whom we, in the clear perception of faith and obedience, may see to-day. We mean that the fullest light, the truest light, the light most eternal and unchanging which can shine upon our human problems is that which shines from God through Him whose soul was the mightiest window ever lifted into the temple of the soul of man.

Remembering, then, those values of light which we have already considered, let us think of the light of God in Jesus.

Without the light which comes from the accepted presence of Jesus, our world to-day is full and shall be full of those vague and growing terrors which the primitive mind or the child mind or the broken and weakened mind associates with the dark. We have let loose in our time many of the primitive impulses. We have smashed the ladders of civilized habits of mind and body by which men had slowly climbed to higher levels of behavior, and have let the human spirit tumble back to claw and struggle for existence down in the morass of primeval savagery. Europe, through decade after decade, bred

15

W. Russell Bowie, D.D.

the war fever while we sat by unheeding and uncaring. Upon the garden of a decent life, ordered for humanity in reasonable peace and plenty by the labors and sacrifices of unnumbered generations, we sowed again the seeds of the jungle, and the jungle returning upon that garden bids fair in wide portions of the world to draw great nations back into the dark allurement of its ignorance, its naked ferocity, its witchcraft of slaughter and blood. Even stout-hearted men come back from Europe almost in despair. They can see no way out for France, for Germany, for Russia. Instead of rebuilding what the War has wrecked, great sections of Europe seem to be slipping slowly down deeper into the morass. The constructive motives, out of which alone a preeminently satisfying human order might be built, are paralyzed. In Philip Gibbs's *More That Must Be Told,* there is a notable paragraph in which he sets forth the failure of European civilization before the War to rise to such effective mobilization of the higher human motives as might have prevented the development of that catastrophe:

The old men of Europe (not old in years, but in traditions) made never an effort to tame the wild beast in the heart of Germany (or in their own), never once raised ideals to which the German people might rise with a sense of liberty and brotherhood from the spell of Junkerdom. They made no kind

16

of effort to get European civilization out of the jungle darkness to new clearing places of light. They were all in the jungle together. A friend of mine with bitter cynicism compared the international politicians before the War with ape-men, peering out of their caves, gibbering and beckoning to friendly apes, frothing and mouthing to hostile apes, collecting great stores of weapons for defense and offense, strengthening the approaches to the monkey rooks, listening with fear to the crashing of the Great Ape in the undergrowth of his own jungle, whispering together with a grave nodding of heads, a plotting of white hairs, while the young apes played among the trees with the ignorance and carelessness of youth.

Terrible that metaphor confessedly is, and drawn with the bold strokes of impassioned feeling. Yet exaggerated and extreme though it appear, it is true, as Philip Gibbs goes on to say, that if the European system were put into the parable of the animal world by the spirit of Æsop, or of Swift, or of La Fontaine, it is with jungle life or with ape-life that it could only be compared. Is it not true that, as we regard the international danger points of the world to-day, the trouble grows out of the fact that there is no clear light by which men see and shape their policy—no wide, beneficent, kindly understanding which includes all the elements of reality and reconciles them in some magnanimous truth? Civilization cannot be redeemed by fattening the reptile or the animal in the policies of nations. As God looks down upon the earth to-day, it must be with the infinite and wistful pitifulness of an understanding which sees the folly of that imagined shrewdness which would be ridiculous if it were not so sad.

It is not that the men who before or since have led and may lead great nations down old, bloody highroads of disaster, are bad men. No, not that. Often they are full of the conventional virtues of the would-be patriot. They are lovers of their country who sincerely want to advance and maintain what they imagine to be the interests of their peoples. They are not bad men; but they are blind—blind to those mightier truths which are deeper and more far-reaching than little shrewd schemes of temporary prudence and advantage; blind to those far certainties of moral cause and effect which bring their ultimate vengeance on those who dare defy them. They have looked out upon their world in a kind of light, but a narrow and misleading one—a baleful light of common plots, and fierce and disingenuous stratagems. The awful realities of these years have made it plain that such light as that is only darkness. The supposed wisdom of diplomats, plotting selfishly for their own countries, has been worse than foolishness. It has led the world down into the dark pit of disaster, and bids fair to thrust it there again in these fateful years when the better instincts of the war-weary millions are reaching up for something better.

The Revealing Light

In those same letters of Franklin K. Lane to which we have already once referred, there is another fine statement of his worth remembering. "We have," he writes, "lost all traditional moorings. We have no religion. We have no philosophy. We are materialists because we have no faith. This thing, however, is being changed. We are coming to recognize spiritual forces, and I put my hope for the future, not in any scheme of government, but in the recognition by the people that, after all, there is a God in the world." What is that but to say in another fashion what the Psalmist has put in that immortal phrase, "In thy light shall we see light"? Our world must find God, if it would find the way through chaos and confusion out into the decent security of an ordered and peaceful life. It must find God as revealed in the face of Jesus Christ. It must remember that the greatness of nations will not consist in any conscious manipulation, by greed or violence, of commercial profit, in financial aggrandizement or extent of territory and military influence. The greatness of a nation must consist in the spirit of a people set free from brutal self-seeking on the one hand and from fear on the other, to develop its own genius in kindliness and confidence. This can never be attained except in a world where each people remembers that its welfare is bound

19

up indissolubly with the welfare of all humanity, and remembers, too, that there can be no ultimate security for any people except in a world which is ordered for the good of all. The only practical hope for our civilization to-day is that which fools would call impracticable. It is a new spirit, mastering the conscience of a people and reflected from them in their public servants, a new spirit which will try deliberately to bring the mind of Christ to the ordering of our distracted age.

When men and nations begin to emphasize less their supposed rights and to think more deliberately of their duties; when they ask not only what they owe to their people's benefit, but what they owe to God; when they shape tariffs and formulate foreign policies and regulate the dealings of their citizens, not with the sinister regard of those who look out upon the world to see only what they can get, but with the wide vision of those who see that, in this human complex whose laws are made by God, only those shall finally gain who try to *serve* and *give* —then we shall set our feet on the road that leads to the better day. Great nations have tried to make a civilization by selfishness; by greed; by the self-sufficiency that leads to violence as Germany's did, or the self-sufficiency that merely shuts itself in callous isolation, as ours would do to-day; but these things which the vanity of small minds account to be wisdom have only been the marsh-lights that led, and will lead, into the swamps. What is needed now is the real light that can come only from religion. Mankind will be saved, not by Mars and not by Mammon, but by Christ. Redemption will come, not from the mailed fist nor from the clutch of any avaricious fingers, but only from the touch of the wounded hands.

III

If we need the light of God to deliver our world from its fears and from all the dangers hiding in the present darkness of its organized hatred, so we need the light of God to deliver us from those nearer perplexities that beset men and women in this time. The War affected not only our international relationships, but much of the realm of personal conduct as well. It dislocated old ways of thought. It called out a certain fierce primitiveness in men and women which once released is not easily tamed. It clothed itself in the plausible terms of a new psychology and philosophy. The personality must be free, we are told, from inhibitions. The great thing is for the man and woman to express to the full their own natural urge for unhampered life. That is the new

21

light in which we are to see light to-day. Old ideas of morality, of faithfulness in family life, of self-discipline, and fine obedience to something more authoritative than immediate desire are alleged to be out of date. Contemporary books and the contemporary drama are full of the suggestion that the old guide-post must be turned away from if the new road to freedom is to be found.

There are a great many people around us to-day who have deliberately given up all sense of a religious leading for their lives. They do as they please from day to day. Some of them are nothing but common sensualists, hiding under large words the fundamental indecency of lives that are a continual dishonor. More of them have the instinctive integrity which keeps them from moral disintegration, but they too may be lazy, self-indulgent, useless. They contribute no saving earnestness to the communities in which they live, or rather they hardly live in any community at all, but simply move indifferently between one place and another, according to the convenience of the season and their own restless caprice, sending down no roots of loyal attachment into any surroundings, taking by the power of money, which in most cases they themselves did not earn, the most extravagant luxuries which the world can give, and making no contribution of service in return. Cities

of America which call themselves Christian have
their multitudes of these people who in their outlook
on life are as crudely pagan as though such a thing
as spiritual conviction had no existence in the world.

Nevertheless, the old words of the Psalmist come
with an accent that is stronger and more enduring
than the chatter by which the vain and shallow try
to assert the modern distinction of being worthless.
The trouble with the selfish lives is that the light of
the supposed instincts which they imagine they can
follow plays them false. It does not lead to any
lasting satisfaction, but only into the entanglements,
disappointments, and ultimate disgust. There are
men and women around us whose lives seem out-
wardly to have all that might make for happiness.
They have wealth, leisure, social opportunity; but
they are cursed with inward wretchedness. Their
faces reveal it. Their own hearts know it. They have
looked at life in false perspective. They need to
see it in the light of God. They must measure their
self-indulgence against the strong self-mastery of
Jesus, their parasitic indolence against His heroic
and joyous will to serve, their moody pathways of
capricious impulse against the clean, firm road of
conviction which He would help them build. Are
there not some who listen in this place to-day who
know that they belong to those whom I describe?

23

W. Russell Bowie, D.D.

Is it not true that you have groped in the twilight of a deliberate ungodliness, and that you find your feet now in the quicksand of bewilderment? You have sought your own self-pleasing, and it has led you round in a restless circle back to the same point of emptiness from which you started. You have tried to appropriate for yourself all the flowers of this world's richness and beauty; but blunderingly you have only trampled upon the stems that grew them, and the garden to-day is dead beneath your feet. The twilight of your disillusionment falls about you, and you do not know which way to turn. And yet you do know too. You need to turn to the light of God in the face of Jesus Christ, to see His gentleness and His beauty, His high meaning for the life that so easily we make common, His better ways of dedication in which He means that you should walk!

Finally, as light means safety and means guidance, so, as we have remembered, it means color and growth, for things which otherwise would be dark and dead.

If that is so with the landscape of the visible world, so also it is true with the landscape of the spirit. For the most part, life's beauty must come, if it comes at all, from the common and familiar things. For some these have no freshness of suggestion, no thrill and loveliness of new surprise. Work is to them a drab monotony, friendship a dull matter of fact, even love of wife or child or husband or mother a thing which through long acceptance has become common. It is as though a cataract had formed on the eyes of the spirit. Realities which ought to be full of infinite variety and loveliness are seen as in a dull, gray fog. The world of life and love is like some island in a sea of darkness to which the sunshine never comes.

Whence does the sunshine come? It comes from the consciousness of God. Again in the simplest and most familiar experiences, even as in the greatest and most far-reaching problems of the world, the old sweet words are true, "In thy light shall we see light." Let the consciousness of God be born within the human soul, let it lift itself on the horizon like the dawn, and instantly all the objects which before were commonplace are bathed in the new suggestion. The work which perhaps was a dull thing indifferently regarded becomes the trust of God which must be discharged with honor. The petty vexations of the day, its minor duties, its interruptions with their trial to the temper, become also a part of God's opportunity for the spirit's growth. The comradeship of friends, the trust of little children, the love of men and women, become ennobled because the heart, through God, is lifted to nobler capacity for appreciation and affection. All human beings become more honorable, and even the common contacts of the street and shop and the work-room become more inspiring because the light of the thought of God, shining on those other lives, clothes them with significance. In His light we see the light in them.

"For ye were sometimes darkness," wrote St. Paul. Is that true, perhaps, of many of us who think together now? Darkness of fear, of bewilderment, of the needless lack of color in the life that ought to be so colorful and lovely and inspiring? "But now," St. Paul goes on, "are ye light in the Lord." That is the promise of the truth which we can claim if, as eager watchers facing toward the dawn, we cry for the coming of the glory of God. His presence will rise, like the sun, to fill the earth and sky with radiance. "In his light shall we see light."

THE PRICE OF THE BEST

Dr. Atkins was born in Indiana in 1868, educated at Ohio State University, and after graduating from the Cincinnati School of Law, studied in Yale Divinity School—entering the Congregational ministry in 1895. Two ministries in New England preceded his first pastorate in the First Church of Detroit, 1906-10, to which he returned after seven years in the Central Church of Providence: an unusual thing to do and rather dangerous, but, happily, in this instance an exception to all rules. How well I recall a winter day when I read his *Pilgrims of the Lonely Road*, enthralled equally by its knowledge of the shadowy path by which man finds his way to God, and by the lovely lengths of haunting prose in which so many cadences are gathered and bidden to linger. Since then I have read everything he has written, from *The Godward Side of Life* to *An Undiscovered Country;* and in each book there is the same richness of matter and distinction of manner. Yes, "distinction" is the word to describe all his work. Who else among us could have written *A Rendezvous with Life,* interpreting the Seeger line in terms of daily task and opportunity, and in a fashion hardly less picturesque. Nor would it be easy to name another who could have dealt with the variegated assortment of *Modern Religious Cults and Movements* with such wise sympathy and understanding, making it one of the best pieces of work since William James went away. This sermon is typical of his genius in its clarity of insight, its quiet urgency of appeal, and the gem-bright beauty of style with which he tells us of "the Pearl of Eternity," to use a phrase of an old mystic, "for which a man may gladly give all that he possesses and which he may buy for no less a price."

THE PRICE OF THE BEST

GAIUS GLENN ATKINS, D.D.

FIRST CONGREGATIONAL CHURCH, DETROIT

"Again, the kingdom of heaven is like unto a merchant man, seeking goodly pearls: who, when he had found one pearl of great price, went and sold all that he had, and bought it." Matt. 13: 45, 46.

This text is taken from one of a group of parables in which Jesus appraises and illustrates the worth and character of the Kingdom of Heaven. He never really defines it. A definition is a wall we build around a word to get its meaning within some understandable space, and walls have their limitations.

> Before I build, I would ask to know
> What I was walling in, or walling out,
>
> .   .   .   .   .   .
>
> Something there is that does not love a wall,
> That wants it down.

The greatest things cannot thus be shut in. You may fence a piece of ground, but never the winds which blow across it, nor the drifting shadows of the clouds above it. No more can you fence the Kingdom of Heaven with a definition.

29

But Jesus is constantly approaching it from every side, suggesting values, relationships, analogies, illustrating and exalting it till its massive contours lie against the horizons of the Gospels as Mt. Blanc from Chamonix. In the 13th chapter of St. Matthew it is the field in which seed is planted, and the seed which is sown; it is the leaven which transforms and the treasure which men seek, and, above all, it is the "pearl of great price" for which a man may gladly give all that he possesses and which he may buy at no less a price.

The Century Dictionary defines "best" as "whatever is of the highest quality, excellence or standing; it is said of both persons and things in regard to mental, moral, or physical qualities, whether inherent or acquired." An inclusive definition that, covering almost everything, but it fails, as our fences fail to shut in the sky. For the best belongs to the ranges of the ideal, bafflingly indefinite, irresistibly compelling; it is a region of dreams and desires whose light is drawn from far and mystic sources, where a man may quickly lose himself or mistake a mirage for living water, but into which he is bound to adventure for all that, or else stop short in the journey of life.

We all want the best, but differ strangely in our understandings of it. One man's best is often enough another man's worst. One man's best keeps him under his own roof-tree, another man's best makes him a wanderer beneath the stars. The saint's best is his soul and the best of the libertine is his appetites. The best of the scholar is knowledge and the best of the money-getter is gold. The best of the artist is beauty, the musician's best is song. Cæsar's best is a throne and Jesus' best is a cross, and yet for all such as these the best is a light or a lure, an outer excellence or an inner perfection in whose quest a man may spend himself utterly and in whose possession all his dreams come true.

It would seem, therefore, that if we might achieve amongst us a right understanding of the best and create within us the willingness to pay the price of it, we should have discovered the secret of the triumphant conduct of life. But it is impossible to separate these two conditions, for the power to know the best is also part of its price and we shall come directly to the heart of the whole great matter by a bit of analysis. The price of the best is, first: the power to know it; second: the capacity to labor for it; third: the willingness to surrender the lesser good for the sake of it.

Gaius Glenn Atkins, D.D.

I

Plato, who also considered such things as these, believed that we are come into this present world out of some preëxistent state where truth and beauty and goodness were the perfect laws of a perfect life and what is here the disturbing aspiration of our souls was the glad possession of those who had no dreams because every dream was reality. Something of the recollection of this we have brought with us through the narrow gates of rebirth. Because the gates are so narrow we have been able to bring with us but little of what we then had and then were, but, none the less, we have brought something. "Trailing clouds of glory we have come," and all our visions, splendid as they are and greatly as they compel us, are but the haunting memories of an existence so splendid and an order so radiant that one broken recollection of it all is enough to fill our world with glory.

This is only a poet's dream, the baseless fabric of the meditation of a philosopher whose mighty service it is to have forever exalted the value of the ideal and to have taught us that we were born for something better than the broken and incomplete, possessing by divine right a citizenship in a "better, that is a Heavenly country."

The Price of the Best

What Plato sought in the past, Jesus Christ discovers in the future; Plato's perfections are in memory, the perfections of Christ in faith and sacrifice and hope. The sources of Plato's better world are hid in the mists which lie across the land of dreams; the sources of the best for Jesus Christ are in the nature and power of God. This power of ours to build in vision and imagination a better world, and to discern beyond what we are the glory of what we may become, is what is nearest to God in the human soul.

Some of us have a power to apprehend and make manifest the best which is denied the commonalty of folk. Such as these are more sensitive to the enduring values; they possess insights and understandings which are denied the rest of us; they hear more clearly some accent of the Holy Ghost; indeed, we only wrap the matter up in words as we go on saying such things as this. It is better to use illustrations. A thousand painters have painted the faces of old men and women, but only Rembrandt has been able to give tired eyes their haunting look of eternal longing, and depict on lined faces the sorrow, the dignity, and the indefinable wonder of our common life.

We shall never know why Beethoven and Wagner and Handel were able to hear in their silences those

harmonies to which the rest of us are deaf, and so
voice them in symphonies and Pilgrim Choruses and
haunting arias as to make their music like the sound
of many waters or viewless tides which bear us out,
as we commit ourselves to them, into regions whose
pleasures are without material suggestion and whose
realities belong neither to space nor to time. We do
not know how Watts was able to paint love and life
and death in such majestic and moving guise that
the galleries which house his canvases become a
temple and our souls confess the magic of the
painter's brush.

We do not know how St. Gaudens models a Shaw
Memorial or an Abraham Lincoln any more than
we know how Tennyson was inspired to sing of
"Sunset and evening star," or Ruskin to write a
prose which is luminous with mountain glory or
somber with mountain gloom, or echoes the music
of Alpine streams, or recreates the magic of Swiss
meadows starred with flowers. But, by the grace
of God, these men and their comrades have been
able to do such things and so they have created for
us the best of music and literature and art, as the
scholars and philosophers have created for us the
best of truth and knowledge and as the saints have
created for us the best of conduct and character.

And if we do not possess within ourselves the

power to create as they have created, or to see as
they have seen, we nevertheless do possess the
power of being taught and disciplined by them.
There is something within us which responds to
what they have seen and done as there was a
supreme excellency in them which responded to
what God had revealed and done. So we shall
know the best as we dwell much in their fellowship and take counsel with those who have been its
prophets or the living incarnation of it. This is
what schools are for and the whole process of education, and not a little of the fault of modern
education lies in its failure in just these regions.

For what shall it profit a man to understand the
higher mathematics and to have been made a master
of technical processes if, at the same time, he does
not understand the power of love and faith and
goodness and has no vision of the true ends to which
his skill must address itself? But when we do let
the best have its way with us, dwelling much in the
comradeship of it, open to its suggestions and
obedient to its voices, then, by the grace of God,
we being what we are and the best what it is, it
will in the end make us its disciples.

For the best needs time and much living with.
It does not take us by storm, it wins us slowly by
the beauty, grace, or wonder of it, displacing lesser

things by its majestic self-assertion, establishing its
sovereignty in our own consent and fashioning us to
become its ministers or its habitations before it sets
up its throne room in our souls. I cannot sufficiently illustrate all this, though there is no end of
illustration. Take music for example. Our first
hearing of a great symphony was often a weary
experience. Its themes and hesitant harmonies, its
intricate movements and embroidered variations
were too high and hard for us.

We did not understand how harmony gathers
melody into its movements as some great stream
carries along with it all its tributaries. But in the
end great music often heard began to have its way
with us. It created new powers of appreciation,
new faculties of understanding, set up its own
standards and ruled by its own laws. Poor music
and cheap and noisy fell back into its own low place
and we saw that between a noble rendering of a
noble symphony and the last popular song there is
an almost unbridgeable gulf. So we were made free
of the best, friends and lovers of it rejoicing in the
greatness of it, answering to the call of it and anticipating in the glory of it that music which the seer
of the Book of Revelation heard beating like the
waves of the sea at the foot of the throne of God.

What is true of training in music is true also of

training in art and architecture and supremely true
of growth in character and conduct and fellowship.
There is always, for every task and every relationship, a best. Sometimes very simple, as a motor
car or carrying on a business. Sometimes rare and
high as the best way of lifting the fretted towers of
time-worn cathedrals against the sky, or organizing
the State, or perfecting the soul. But all these
things, small or great, have something in common,
some suggestion of excellence, some satisfying appeal to the eye or the heart or the soul, some inti-
mation of "a spirit still more deeply interfused"
which, whether it reveal itself in the weaving of a
piece of cloth or the fabrication of character, is still
the same spirit facing us in the same direction and
revealing to us a supreme power.

The best is always honest and always useful;
there is something of love in it and something of
service; it is true in proportion; it has its elements
of beauty; it always looks away from the stained
and the commonplace; it is always calling us to
something better still than itself; it at once satisfies
us and fills us with divine discontent. Step by step
the best builds for us the ladders by which we climb
and I care not where you are or what you are doing,
if you have only the vision of the best in your station and your task it will face you toward God.

Gaius Glenn Atkins, D.D.

The first price of the best is the dearly bought and richly rewarding power to know it.

II

The second price of the best is the capacity to labor for it. It is not enough to recognize it, to know its tests and its laws, to face toward it and to long for it; we must go on to make it real and this means sheer, endless, hard work. It is happy work, I grant you. There is no happiness in life like doing some worthy thing in a fine way. There is a workman within us all who sings at his work when he loves it and does it well. Then we share something of the joy of God and repeat within our souls the splendor of that creative morning in which willing constellations were set in their places and all the stars sang together for joy that they were made. But it means weariness, none the less, a trying capacity for taking pains and the willingness to do over and over again the thing which seemed quite well done, but not quite as well done as it might be.

A hurrying, impatient time, more concerned with quantity than quality of production, a machine-made time and all that goes along with a machine-made time, is not kind to good work. Nearly all

38

our factories have a speeding-up system in which
the man who sets the pace possesses a driving
faculty for rapid mechanical operation; all the rest
in his line take their tempo from him—or leave the
line.   There is no place in such a system for loving
excellency of craftsmanship.   Cathedrals are not
built like that, nor did medieval workmen thus forge
a sword or make a coat of mail or weave a fabric
shot with splendor.   It was not thus that the gold-
smiths of the Renaissance beat out their work, nor
the craftsmen of Greece built their Parthenons.
Perhaps our protests against the mechanics of our
time are vain and we gain in the range of our material comfort what we lose in creative joy—I do
not know.   But I do know that the best demands
something more than sweat-stained piecework.

It demands labor happily done with love and
vision and care.   No one has written such English
as Ruskin at his best.   You may find what fault
with him and his gospel you will, nevertheless there
remain of him passages which constitute and will
always constitute a peculiar treasure of our mother
tongue.   We have, happily, manuscripts of his
which tell us how he did his work, crossed, re-
crossed, interwritten, as it were a tangled web, but
none the less a web woven upon the loom of a master
mind, out of which there finally emerges a golden,

glowing fabric, each new word better than the last, each new sentence more nobly rhythmic, each new image more luminously suggestive, until at last the passage stands before us written as the angels write who keep the books of God. But it was all hard work, sheer hard work.

You read Charles Dickens in endless wonder at the wealth of his imagination and the elasticity of his mind, and yet Dickens' manuscripts are akin to Ruskin's in their revelation of a consuming toil and an almost endless correction. Charles Frederick Watts spent all the later years of his life working over a figure which was to represent Physical Knowledge. Those with whom he lived used to hear the old man laboring in the gray dawn, the sound of his hammer as it were the echo of the ardor of his soul, and, even so, he left the figure unfinished. The great scientists have given their lives to their discoveries; the great statesmen have been men of endless industry; from every region in which excellence, whether simple or great, has ever been achieved, there comes to us a great crowd of witnesses bearing this common testimony that we may purchase the best only at the price of great labor.

The Price of the Best

III

And all this deepens down into something indeed akin to what we have been considering, but something greater still. The price of the best is the willingness to be wholly lost in the achievement of it. Labor and sacrifice are both a fire, but labor is the constant heat of a slow fire, and sacrifice is that fire blown for one splendid and glowing instant into flame. It is in those flaming moments that the great things are consummated and though they consume the one who does the work, none the less he lives in what he has so greatly done and thereafter belongs to the fellowship of the Immortals. This is perhaps only another way of saying that the greater bests come out of flaming passions and intensities. The altar of the best asks for a sacrifice the whole of us, body, mind, and soul. No wonder we fear it. The richer colors of the great canvases are mixed with the heart blood of the men who painted them; the inspiring strains of the great symphonies which lift us so high, carried the men who voiced them altogether and often too soon out of our world.

There is throughout the earlier part of the Old Testament a haunting fear of the vision of God and a strange persuasion that no one could look upon Him and live. So with the best; its lights are blind-

41

ing, its fires are consuming and those who rise to its highest levels pay their price for their seasons of vision and their ecstasy of creation. More than that, there have always been times in human history, as there have always been crises in the human soul, when some great cause which has become for the time the very incarnation of the best has asked of those who would hear and follow, an utter devotion of all that they are. The saints and the mystics have always known this. We purchase our commonplace goodness at the commonplace price, but they paid for sanctity with self-denial and sometimes martyrdom. They poured everything into the crucible and though we have drawn therefrom the pure gold of their spirit, they themselves perished in the flames.

Lovers of the best can never be cautious nor conservative; they must from time to time choose between the lesser interests and the supreme interests. They must decide between the comfortable acceptance of things as they are and the resolute affirmation of things as they ought to be. No need to say where this leads us. It leads us toward the fellowship of the saints and prophets, the apostles and the martyrs—those who were not disobedient unto the heavenly vision and whose obedience, though it cost them so greatly, is the secret of their deathless power. All this is, I confess, a strong statement of situations all of us may not be asked to face, nor any of us, save in those rare and shining moments when the best asks the last great price, but unless there be at the heart of all of our love of the best a passion which will make us equal to any challenge of it, we shall fail of the best even in happy and unheroic times.

IV

I would not for a moment underestimate the high achievement of our own time, nor the passion for the best which holds amongst us. Each age has its own excellencies and many forces conspire to create for changing lands and times some changing splendor of high achievement. Only Egypt could bury its kings in such tombs as Tut-ankh-amen's, only Greece lift the pillared perfectness of the Parthenon against an azure sky, only Rome make a golden mile post the center of empire, only Palestine voice the devotion of humanity in her Psalms. But we have our own virtues and our own visions and they are not unworthy of our time and its force. Perhaps the secret of our discontent is in the range and daring of our dreams. High things are low enough when you measure them against the skyline

43

of the world. We are discontented with many conditions which would doubtless seem to other times the happy realization of their braver dreams, and other times have doubtless shared with us the unwillingness to pay the full price of the best.

But I wonder after all if we may not find in some arresting disparity between our dreams and the practical conduct of our affairs, the secret of our spiritual entanglements. We dream of peace and maintain the most massive armaments of time; we see

> —beyond the years
> "Our" alabaster cities gleam
> Undimmed by human tears.

And yet we darken our skies with smoke till nothing gleams undarkened, and create new occasions for tears in the death toll of our hard-driven motor cars. We pray for the Kingdom of God and build amongst us, still more deeply established in almost every aspect of our human enterprise, the structure of an order alien to the Master's vision, and all because we will not pay the price of our dreams. We can have the better things, not quickly or easily, but always at their price. God is a just paymaster. We have just as much of the best as we deserve, often a little more, never less.

The Price of the Best

The price of alabaster cities is white-souled men and women and clean-handed, high-minded officials and civic coöperation and an intelligent understanding of civic problems and eternal vigilance and foresighted programs and creative patience and the subordination of lesser interests to the common good.

The price of a noble state is a noble citizenship, for whom the state is a revelation of spiritual and ethical values, secured by obedience to law and wise administration and flawless justice and a supreme concern for human and humane conditions in every relationship.

The price of a warless world is a passion for peace and honorable diplomacies and the coöperative creation of an international machinery which will substitute its own decisions and adjustments for the arbitrament of war, and a braver confidence in good will and the care to do no despite to others, and the understanding of the full humanity of folk whose flag is not our flag, whose speech is not our speech—whose skins are not our color. The price of a warless world is new definitions of honor and patriotism, a deepening hatred of hate, a clearer vision of the grim realities behind the seductive pageantry of armies and navies, a new understanding of the fallacy of force, a radiant confidence in the Gospel of

Jesus Christ. The price of a soul is unfailing well-doing, and the mastery of low inheritance, and love and labor and faith undimmed, and hidden fellowship with unseen and enduring things.

And the price of the Kingdom of God? Just what Jesus said—all that a man has. Christianity has always asked everything a man has. It asked of the handful of Jews who first followed Jesus the willingness to be separated from their people and forego their pride. It asked of Greeks and Romans who made the cross their sign, the willingness, at a cost which we shall never understand, to disentangle themselves from a pagan life which met and seduced them at every step they made. It asked of our fathers' fathers in northern forests, new reverences, new obediences, new goodnesses.

To-day the Kingdom of God is asking us to apply its principles to the conduct of our common life, to make its spirit regnant in politics and in business, to test our convictions and our inheritances by its tests and to subdue every region of our lives to its imperial concern.

V

Aye, the best has its price, but the best is worth its price. We can at any rate do no more—nor less

—than spend ourselves; life is just a matter of exchange. Here is a lesson from the Parable of the Talents not often considered. God does not ask us to put the treasure of life to the exchanges for His profit, but for ours. The buried life is lost. We have no choice but to trade, our only choice is the market to which we go. We spend the pregnant force of us, body, mind, and soul; we spend our days and our years; we spend our laughter and our tears, our love, our labor, and our rest; the inexorable laws of life demand them all and when we have spent the substance for the shadow, how piteously poor we are. A man takes away a poor profit when he trades at the stalls of Vanity Fair, though he buy himself honors, preferments, titles, countries, kingdoms, lusts, or pleasures.

There is a nobler exchange than that. We may buy knowledge with study, and strength with labor, and tenderness with tears, and high happiness with laughter. We may bring away courage from the field of battle and goodness from much wrestling with evil things. The passing years leave behind them a deposit of rich experience. Love gains added love, and loyalties are paid for in a splendor of holy causes greatly served and a wealth of soul whose glory, like the glory of pictured windows only dimly guessed from without, is their enduring treasure who conduct the commerce of their lives with the best. How superbly are they profited who, having spent all, have gained their own souls and in the gaining of them touched with a rarer glory the fellowships of which they are a part and brought a little nearer the Master's purpose and the prophet's dream.

THE SURVIVAL OF FAITH

Dr. Roberts is a Welshman, a preacher both by nature and by grace, a mystic in his faith and a keen analytical realist in his thought; a teacher suffused with the glow of vision—no blinding flame, no flashing lightning—and a quiet, penetrating spiritual intelligence; as if he had wrestled with the questions which fever men, but waited till the fevers were past. Educated in his native land, he came from a notable pastorate in Crouch End, London, to the Church of the Pilgrims in Brooklyn, and thence to his throne of power in the American Church of Montreal—one of the most strategic and influential pulpits in our Western World. His books best known in America are *That One Face,* a study of Jesus in the minds of poets and prophets, and his searching critique of modern life in the light of the mind of Jesus, in *The Untried Door.* But some of us like best *The Papers of John Pererin,* published anonymously, if only because that wise man knew, with Patmore, that "in divinity and love what's best worth saying can't be said." The value of this sermon, apart from its devastating analysis of the dogma of automatic evolution, lies in its emphasis upon the need of effort, discipline, method in the culture of the inner life, lest faith fade from our hearts in the rush of activity and the cumber of neglect. Oddly enough, we who insist upon system in everything try to live the spiritual life haphazard, and it is a wonder that we have any faith at all, since we take so little time and pains to keep it alive and aglow in our hearts.

THE SURVIVAL OF FAITH

RICHARD ROBERTS, D.D.

THE AMERICAN CHURCH, MONTREAL

"When the Son of man cometh, shall he find faith on the earth?" Luke 18: 8.

I

I imagine that most of us have stood and pondered over this verse. Was it a passing mood of pessimism? Was it a momentary failure of nerve? Or was it perhaps pure weariness of mind and body, the sort of condition in which we all sink into doubt and misgiving about the future? Or was it the deliberate expression of an abiding and reasoned conviction? At first sight it seems somewhat strange that Jesus, whose faith in God was so sure and serene, should have had any doubts. But, plainly, it is one thing to have faith in God and quite another to have faith in man. And explain this how you will, it does reflect a skepticism about human nature.

Obviously, Jesus did not believe in Progress—in the inevitability of human perfection. This passage itself is enough to prove that Jesus did not think

51

that the world would necessarily grow better and finer. And the sooner we rid ourselves of the nineteenth-century myth of Progress, the better for us and for the world. "Always toward perfection is the mighty movement," cried Herbert Spencer in a dithyrambic moment; and because the prediction was made in the name of Science, we swallowed it whole, not knowing that science no less than Religion could have its superstitions. The doctrine of evolution was extended into the theory that there was an irresistible force behind us driving us onward to some indefinable splendor of perfection; and the entirely sound doctrine of human perfectibility was transfigured into the wholly false doctrine of the certainty of human perfection.

And in those days there were some sanctions for the illusion. Great strides were actually being made in knowledge and invention; it did seem as though the growth of modern science with its continuous conquest of the world of nature indicated a forward movement of so great promise as to persuade us that its momentum was inexhaustible. But we were over-credulous; we lacked realism of insight; for while all this alleged progress was going on before our eyes, we were so dazzled by it that we forgot to take account of things that were going on out of sight. And it took the terrible apocalypse of War to show us that all this time we were living in a fool's paradise. For with all its external progress, the world was growing rotten at heart; with all its mechanical and physical triumphs, it was in a condition of spiritual and moral decadence. Mr. C. F. G. Masterman, speaking of the present state of the world, says in a recently published book: "This is not a collapse of the European Faith caused by the war; it is collapse revealed by the war." For us of this generation, to whom the confusion and sorrow of nearly ten years have shown beyond forgetting the perverseness and stupidity of human nature and who will carry the scars of its wounds upon our souls to the grave, it should not be difficult to enter into the thought of Jesus when he asked his ominous question—"When the Son of man cometh, shall he find faith upon the earth?"

II

With the word Progress went another which we did not sufficiently examine—the word *Civilization*. There is, to be sure, nothing wrong with the word; the mischief is in the sort of content we have given to it. A recent writer draws a distinction between civilization and culture. Culture, he says, "is the complex of all the inner and spiritual values of mankind (religion, art, philosophy)," and Civilization is "the sum of all the external values (industry, technics, trade, politics, etc.)." He goes on to point out that culture and civilization do not necessarily go together, and gives instances of races which have had a high culture with a meager civilization, and of others who have had a great civilization with a relatively low culture. And his conclusion is that "the hidden drama of history is an everlasting struggle between the external and the inner values of mankind, a struggle between matter and spirit, between culture and civilization." In this struggle, the odds are in favor of the outer as against the inner, in favor of civilization as against culture.

This, I think, is only a modern way of saying what was in the mind of Jesus; and it is borne out by what students of the history of civilization tell us. Newman, you will remember, held that a civilization began in an age of faith, thence passed into an age of analysis and skepticism, and finally reached an age of materialism. The force of the inner cultural impulse is worn down by the attrition of reason and sense. Faith is hard put to it to survive. And that is not difficult to explain. We are creatures of sense living in a world of things. The objects of faith are remote, impalpable, and imponderable, while the objects of sense are immediate and easily got at.

The Survival of Faith

Faith implies a continuous effort of thought and will to transcend the immediate; and there is in mankind a natural inertia which resists this effort and takes easily and comfortably to the line of least resistance. So little by little the impulse of faith loses its momentum and we drift to the flesh pots.

Now this was the very danger that Jesus had in his mind in the parable of the Importunate Widow, to which this question is a postscript. If the stubbornness of that judge with the hard face and the hard heart could be broken down by the pertinacity of a poor widow, do you think that God will not vindicate his own faithful children? You can, he insists, count upon God to justify those who put their trust in him, to vindicate those who live in the spirit and wait for his kingdom. If human nature at its worst (and the picture of the impious and inhuman judge is meant to suggest that) can be prevailed upon to redress a grievance by the sheer importunity of an injured and friendless widow, then it stands to reason that God will not allow those who look to him to be confounded.

There is a word in the parable from which the text is taken which seems to involve an inconsistency, "I tell you he will avenge them speedily." *Speedily*, you will observe. Now, in the parable the point is plainly that the dilatoriness of the judge is overcome

by the perseverance of the widow, and that is intended to hint at the fact that God also takes his
time about vindicating the faith of the elect. That
is indeed one of the commonplaces of the religious
experience; God does not always come to the rescue
of his own speedily. He seems to take his time about
it; and that is why the effort of faith becomes so
heavy to maintain. That was the ground of the
Jewish pessimism in Babylon; it is the central point
of the Book of Job. And all through the ages, persons and peoples in long continued distress have
echoed and reëchoed the Psalmist's cry, How long?
O Lord, how long? So that it is not true to experience to say that God is sure to vindicate his elect
speedily. Either the word has crept in by some
inadvertence; or we are to take it as signifying that
though the vindication may be delayed, yet when it
does come it will be swift and summary. And the
problem of the elect is how they are to hold out until
the vindication comes.

III

But before I come to that, I want to say a word
about the realism of Jesus. He had no illusions about
human nature. He knew what was in man and
needed that no man should tell him. He told men

that there was a good time coming; the Kingdom of heaven, he said, is at hand. But it was with none of that shallow optimism which sings that "there's a good time coming," anyhow, and bids us "wait until the clouds roll by." The clouds that overhang human life will not roll by unless we start them rolling; and the Kingdom of heaven comes only to those who repent. You can take God's friendliness, his willingness and readiness for granted; you can count upon that with the most complete confidence. But what Jesus evidently could not count upon was human nature. Not indeed that he ever went to the other extreme of stupid sentimental pessimism which regards human nature as essentially bad and that you cannot change it. Human nature can change; it is changing all the time; and if it is not changing for the better, it is changing for the worse. Of nothing in the world can you say with more assurance that it changes than you can say it of human nature. And it is either improving or deteriorating; the one thing it cannot do is to remain static. But it is not at all sure that the final change in mankind will be for the better. It can be and it may be; but whether it will, no one can tell. And Jesus did not try to tell. He came to redeem mankind; but would mankind allow itself to be redeemed? He came to bring in the Kingdom of God; but would mankind admit the Kingdom into their hearts? And to that question he offered no answer. He believed in the perfectibility of man; but he did not, for he could not affirm the certainty of human perfection. This is a region in which you cannot count on evolution or progress; for man is the arbiter of his own fate. God made him free and put the choice in his own hands. Here there is neither certainty nor inevitability; and Jesus did not suffer himself to be deceived. He said that there was a doubt; but he also believed that there was a hope. And that is the only position which a man who faces all the facts of life can take up. And to-day as we see how little men have assimilated the wisdom that the War made plain as daylight and how the peoples are still building the house of life on the old rotten foundations, are we unreasonable if we believe with Jesus that the destiny of mankind is still in doubt?

IV

In the end, however, we shall have to answer for ourselves, not for mankind. It is indeed true that the circle of our responsibility has a wider radius than we suppose; we are our brothers' keepers to a much greater extent than we commonly recognize. But even then, our central and critical responsibility lies

58

in what we do with ourselves, whether *we* keep faith with the Son of man; and the answer is within our own choice. We can keep the faith if we will. But all the same it is not an easy matter. For faith has to make an endless fight for its life against sense and reason. It has to maintain itself in the face of the confusion and sorrow and distress of life. And if it is left to shift for itself, the pressure of the immediate and outward facts of life will soon or late surely put it out of business. Faith can only survive by continual reaffirmation; if we are to save it alive, we shall have to go out of our way, to take time and trouble to declare ourselves for it. We dare not let it go unwatched and untended. Sense and reason will crowd it out if they can; and when that threatens to happen, and sense and reason are outstepping their province, then we must needs affirm our faith in their teeth—but always taking care that faith for its own sake neither denies nor flouts them nor drives them out of their legitimate places. The facts of life may sometimes threaten to overwhelm our faith; and then faith must nail its colors to the mast in the face of them. And not only in such emergencies as these, when faith is hard beset, but at all times must we take pains to affirm our faith. For even deadlier than the crises and the contradictions of life is the slow imperceptible attrition of the daily round. Jack

London in one of his stories tells of some people in the Arctic Circle who could not see the sun because of the bulge of the earth; and against the bulge of the world which is always too much with us, we must continually constrain faith to bear its testimony to the unseen Sun of our souls.

So we must provide for it in the plan of our lives. The reinforcement and nurture of faith cannot be left to odd moments and to our loose ends of time. In the sort of life we moderns live, faith will be surely crowded out if we do not make for it a place and keep that place inviolate. The idea of the "retreat" springs out of a perfectly sound understanding of the psychology of the inner life; the soul must have its retreats if faith is to live. You remember the seed that fell among thorns; it sprouted; but in that hedgerow there was a struggle for existence and the sensitive slender shoot had no chance. And that is a parable of the crowded life we lead. The word of God is sown in us; and it sprouts in a frail and tender plant of faith. And tough shrubs of secular interest crowd in upon it and choke it so that it withers and dies. So some ground must be cleared and reserved for it. Faith is always under sentence of death in the soul which has no trysting place with the Unseen.

And this trysting place must be sacred and inviolate; the soul's private demesne that is not to be invaded or appropriated by any other concern whatsoever—an hour, or half an hour or even a quarter, staked out in some part of the day and kept religiously to its purpose, when the soul can gather itself together and return to the base of its life; and that become as strong a habit as your lunch hour—that is what I mean by clearing the ground for faith. And remember that perseverance, steadfastness, is of the very essence of the matter. We must regard it for what it is—grave momentous business not to be lightly intruded upon; and we must not suppose any secular call to be of so great urgency as to entitle us to neglect it. More, I think, depends—not alone for ourselves, but for the world —than we can think on our acquiring this habit of the daily retreat of the soul; for our own quickened faith will be a contagious thing, quickening the faith of others. I do not forget that our Sunday Worship is also a retreat of the soul; and we come to the Sacrament as to a trysting place with the Unseen; and all this should go to the renewal of faith "until He come." But beneath and before all our common trysting places, we must first of all recreate the soul's own sanctuary, its own daily resort into the secret place of the Most High. . . .

But, having arrived there, what will it do? There

is indeed plenty to do, as we shall find when we become familiar with the ground. But chiefly this, I imagine; we shall *recollect*—gather together in our thought—those grounds of faith that the day's work may overlay and drive out of our remembrance. We shall think of Jesus—that one clear unsetting star above the confusion of life; we shall think of the Cross, of its judgment upon our worldly standards and our secular blindness; and its unveiling of the divine compassion upon our human failures. We shall think of saints and prophets who esteemed the reproach of Christ greater riches than the treasures of Egypt. We shall think of the great travail of God in creation and in the evolution of life, and of the splendor of that purpose for which he created the soul of man, that purpose which is obstructed by the perversity of man. We shall lift up our eyes on high and dwell in thought upon the vast spaces of a divine providence that sustains this scheme of things, silent and unsleeping. We shall turn the pages of Holy Writ and find here and there a word that opens a window upon immeasurable reaches of life—stretching out far beyond the horizons of sight and sense. And out of its recollection the soul will stand up and declare its faith. . . .

"I believe in the love of God through Jesus Christ.

The Survival of Faith

"I believe in the Cross of Calvary as the ground plan of the Universe.

"I believe in the transcendental meaning and hope of Life.

"I believe that the true goods of life lie in the unseen, where Christ sitteth at the right hand of God, where neither moth nor rust doth corrupt nor thieves break through and steal.

"I believe that the real values of life are the good, the true, and the beautiful.

"I believe in the salvability and the immortality of every man; and in the infinite value of every living soul.

"I believe in the practicability of the Kingdom of God, and in my freedom to choose it and to work for it.

"I believe in the sacramental quality of my day's work, and that I may see and serve God in it.

"I believe in a grace that can overcome my selfishness and my pride, that will enable me to overcome temptation, and upon which I need never call in vain.

"I believe in love as the final law of life.

"And in this faith, by the help of God, I mean to live this day and all my days."

And, men and women, believe me, it is altogether impossible for you or for me to measure what difference such a daily act of faith may make to our days, and to those with whom we have to do. And best of all is this, that whether the master of the house comes at even or at midnight or at cockcrow or in the morning, he shall find us unsleeping, with the banner of our faith flying bravely in the breeze. And whether we shall be of this company of unsurrendered faith or not, it is for us ourselves to say.

THE SALT OF THE EARTH

Dr. Sockman is an outstanding example of the New Preaching in which the old verities of faith are united with a realistic vision of the complexities of modern life, with its problems, obligations and opportunities for larger service. An Ohioan by birth, trained in Ohio Wesleyan College, in Columbia University, and Union Theological Seminary, since 1917 he has been minister of the Madison Avenue Methodist Church of New York City. His first volume of sermons, *Suburbs of Christianity,* recently published—an appeal to those who live on the outer edges of the City of God to come into the City itself, where the real business of faith is done—attracted wide attention, as much for its method as for its message. Simple, direct, rich in sympathy and radiant in faith, with no filigree oratory, it is intimate in its insight, practical in its approach, and searching in its word of comfort and command. The following sermon is typical of a ministry which gives great promise of wise and constructive leadership in a confused and difficult time.

THE SALT OF THE EARTH

RALPH W. SOCKMAN, D.D.

MADISON AVENUE METHODIST CHURCH, NEW YORK

"Ye are the salt of the earth; but if the salt have lost its savor, wherewith shall it be salted? It is thenceforth good for nothing but to be cast out and trodden under foot of men."

Matt. 5: 13.

Jesus recognized man's desire to distinguish himself. The normal person does not wish to be lost in the crowd. On the ladders not only of ambition but of self-respect men climb up to write their names on the walls of society above the reach of the erasing masses. It is not good for a man to lose the sense of his personal distinction under the dwarfing pressure of numbers.

In *The Boy and the Angel* Browning pictures an archangel coming down to sing God's praise in the place of a little boy. The poet interprets God as saying, "I miss my little human praise." Not even the great organ notes of the archangel could replace in the ear of God the tiny treble of the little lad. In God's hearing every human voice has its distinctive tone. A man must recognize this truth if he is to do his best work. He must feel that he is making a unique contribution to society. He must sense his individual worth.

Jesus, therefore, the master developer of individuality, appealed to this human trait. He went to the plain man on the street, so buried in mediocrity that he was overlooked by the temple officials and the governmental authorities. Jesus bade him consider the sparrow, the commonest of birds, the little drab brown creature seemingly so lacking in distinctiveness. "Are not two sparrows sold for a penny? and not one of them shall fall on the ground without your Father; but the very hairs of your head are all numbered. Fear not, therefore: ye are of more value than many sparrows." Hearing that, the little fellow in the crowd straightened up with a new sense of self-respect. He felt himself to be a worth-while actor on the stage of life, for he was under the spotlight of at least God's gaze.

This service rendered by Jesus to the common man in Jerusalem is more imperatively needed for the man in the crowd to-day. As human beings become more compressed in society, the individual must struggle the harder to keep from being submerged in the mass. The crowded city tends to smother individuality. The virtues of the man on Broadway are allowed to blush unseen by appreciative neighbors. His vices can go unblushing because unnoticed by neighborhood censors. The city dweller lacks the support of local reputation to carry him across his moods of waywardness and irresponsibility. It would be hard to estimate how the moral and civic tone of our city communities would be elevated if the residents of a metropolis felt the same sense of personal worth and responsibility as do the dwellers in the diminutive county seat. Cultivating hardy characters is difficult on paved streets amid trampling throngs.

Modern industry, as well as modern cities, tends to make the individual shrivel. More and more men are coming to work in great groups where they are known by number rather than by name. In modern politics, too, the man is becoming increasingly a mere cog in a machine. The citizen of to-day dwells in city ant-hills, works in factory armies, votes in mammoth parties. What can protect the individual from the crowd? What can preserve the uniqueness of the one from the mediocrity of the many?

Our answer is "Religion." We shall be more definitive and say, "The religion of Jesus Christ." The Christian gospel is a gospel of persons, not of percentages. It is the good news of a shepherding Savior who was not content with ninety-nine percent safe, but went out to find the lost one, even though the lone wanderer be the most insignificant unit of America's one hundred millions or of China's four hundred millions. Its results are eloquent. Individual life has been held of more value on the shores of Massachusetts Bay than on the banks of the Ganges. That Christianity which has inflated souls with the spirit of true self-respect is needed more than ever in the crowd pressure of to-day.

"Ye are the salt of the earth," said Jesus; "but if the salt have lost its savor, wherewith shall it be salted?" The followers of Christ must not lose themselves in the crowd. They must retain their distinctive flavor of character and work or be ignored. The Church of Christ is to permeate the world with its influence, but it must not lose its uniqueness. True Christians are the preserving and reasoning element in society, but if they lose their peculiar savor they will forfeit the respect of men and the power of service.

That is the point of the Master's message in our text. That is the burden of the whole fifth chapter of Matthew. In that chapter Matthew has collected certain sayings of Jesus which describe distinctive qualities expected of his followers. They may be roughly grouped for convenience under three general heads. First, a Christian's personal righteousness must "exceed the righteousness" of the crowd. It

The Salt of the Earth

is his extra margin of goodness that makes for the Kingdom of Heaven. Jesus states some of the standardized virtues and vices. "Thou shalt not kill." "Thou shalt not commit adultery." Mere conventional goodness, however, does not make Christians the "salt of the earth."

A college professor was asked recently to name the most subtle and potent evil visible on the horizon of his world. He replied, "Crowd morality." It is a sad sight to watch a lad's lofty peaks of individual virtue leveled down to the mediocrity of the crowd's standards. The college campus often witnesses such moral weathering. It is pathetic to see a young fellow come to a great city from the purity of a godly home with one of those kodak consciences which can take a snapshot of a moral wrong, and then in the foggy atmosphere of some business circles become so dull of vision that he can take a time exposure of a flagrant evil and register only a dull impression. Crowd morality is one of the greatest hindrances of Kingdom progress to-day. "Everybody does it" is a most insidious slogan.

Distinctive goodness is dynamic. A very nice contrast between the merely legalistic virtue that "gets by" in the crowd and the kind of goodness that is dynamic was drawn by The Gentleman with the Duster in *The Glass of Fashion*. The wives of two

71

former British premiers were held up for comparison. One took delight in telling how she flirted with temptations which could never have gotten into the vestibule of the other woman's mind. The same one relates with evident relish how near she could walk to the edge of a moral precipice without falling over. The other, equally vivacious, equally in love with life and society, possessed down underneath her flashing exterior a steadying earnestness of purpose that kept her from all vulgarities. This latter type of virtue helps to quicken the good impulses of others.

Our society has little need for the man of merely legalistic goodness. We have enough of the moral rope-walkers who can tread the taut line of the Ten Commandments without falling off. What we need are the men of surplus virtue who, after they have fought their own temptations, have the energy and desire to help in the struggle of their weaker fellows. We need character giants who can carry their virtues with an easy grace that makes goodness seem attractive and attainable to others. We need men of such abounding moral health that they are immune from sinful infection. It is good to have public officials who will promise to enforce such laws as prohibition, in which they profess not to believe; but we shall have no great measure of success in the enforcement of such laws until we have officials with sufficient social consciousness to desire legislation of this type.

Crowd morality is not dynamic. It is deadly, uninteresting. The romance and flavor of virtue are found in the righteousness which "exceeds the righteousness of the scribes and Pharisees." H. G. Wells has given us a virile figure when he pictures Jesus of Nazareth as a great moral huntsman sweeping across the world, digging men out of the little burrows of respectability in which they have ensconced themselves. What a noble description of Jesus! How he does call men out from their little standardized conceptions of morality! How he summons us to come out beyond the crowd's standards and enjoy the adventure of the "second mile" and "the other cheek."

The Church of Christ must either outrun the crowd in the matter of personal righteousness or be outrun by the crowd and trampled under the foot of men. "Ye are the salt of the earth," said Jesus; "but if the salt have lost its savor, wherewith shall it be salted? It is thenceforth good for nothing but to be cast out and trodden under foot of men."

A second distinctive quality expected of Christians, according to this fifth chapter of Matthew, is speech. The passage beginning, "Thou shalt not forswear thyself," has been used to introduce many a sermon on profanity. Profanity of speech, however, is not limited to the vice commonly called "swearing." The vulgar use of the names of deity is a crudity that, in my opinion, is being outgrown. It is a revelation of a scanty vocabulary. It is a filthy habit that will be removed by the antiseptic of culture.

But Jesus was not referring to that type of profanity merely. He was decrying the popular dilution of current speech with polite insincerities. The scribes and Pharisees had so thinned their language with hypocrisies that they had to thicken it with expletives and oaths to give it any substance of truthfulness. That kind of profanity, I submit, is not being outgrown by cultured society.

The language of business has been corrupted. A homely illustration suffices. Three cartons of eggs stand in a store window. One is labeled "Fresh"; a second, "Strictly Fresh"; a third, "Guaranteed Strictly Fresh." We have multiplied our adjectives and adverbs and, like the German marks, the more they are multiplied the cheaper they become. The language of diplomacy has become synonymous with polite insincerity. When twenty-five years ago John Hay spoke out in straightforward terms, his methods were derisively characterized as "shirt-sleeve diplomacy." The language of the church has been diluted to the point of profanity. A discriminating layman has said recently that a revival of religion could be started in America within a week's time if every minister were to express his religious experiences with the same simple directness that he uses in discussing every-day matters among his friends. Who can deny his assertion? Were not rugged realism and unvarnished simplicity of speech the chief traits of that remarkably dynamic young English preacher, Studdert Kennedy, who a few months ago blessed American audiences with a visit? Are we not to find in sincerity and frankness of language one of the best paths out of the morass of present theological entanglements?

We speak of getting back to apostolic Christianity. Yes, let us return. But let us not go back to the verbose phrase-making theologians of the seventeenth century and call their output apostolic Christianity. Let us not go back to the abstract definitions of creed-making monks of the fourth century and call that apostolic Christianity. Let us return to the simple, direct description of religious experience given by the Master and those who caught the spirit of his message by first-hand contact. Those early followers told what they knew of Jesus in the language of everyday life. The freshness of their story, the directness of their testimony, were contagious. They spread through Mediterranean society. A revival of religion was quickly on. Might not a truly apostolic quickening come to Christianity to-day if we were to reform and rephrase our speech?

"What do ye more than others" in the way of Christ-like realism in speaking? Language is such a truly God-given medium for spirit intercourse. It so often becomes such a man-made non-conductor of truth. Speech is a vital element in that distinctive flavor and preservative power of Christians which make them "the salt of the earth."

A third unique quality expected by Christ of his followers is a superior sense of justice. "An eye for an eye, and a tooth for a tooth" is the crowd's idea of getting even. The Christian must be above that conception.

The traditional figure of Justice as given in art is of a blindfolded woman with a scales in her hand. The essence of justice is thus implied to be the impartial weighing of the evidences in hand. Would the portrayal not become more accurately Christian if the blindfold were removed? It is not enough merely to weigh the facts submitted. To be just one must have insight and imagination to see behind the evidence presented. Hence our courts of justice are coming to have their social investigators, their psycopathic experts. Christian justice, in our private judgments as well as in our public courts, demands that the eyes of our understanding be wide open.

The spirit of justice was expressed with limpid clarity in the Golden Rule. But the application of that Rule in modern complex society is not so simple. If I am to do unto another as I would that he should do unto me, I must know what I should want done unto me were I standing in the other person's place. To put oneself at the other's point of view is the task for the Christianized imagination. Our modern world is being riven with increasing chasms of tragic difference across which it is so hard to see sympathetically. For instance, within the compass of a quarter-mile in our City of New York are to be found apartments with rentals from three thousand to thirty thousand dollars a year, and also tenements with occupants crowded four to a room. Those in the former may wish to be just to those in the latter, but will they give the thought and time sufficient to understand what justice really involves?

If I am to be a just member of economic society I must know something of how life looks to the employer who carries the responsibilities of a great enterprise and also how it looks to the sweated son of toil who stands day after day pulling a lever or blowing a forge. If I am to be a just citizen of America I must be able to understand the sensitivities of a Japanese gentleman and the fears of a French ex-refugee. If I am to exercise my duties justly as a member of the white race I must have insight enough to appreciate the race consciousness of the man whose skin happens to be black or yellow.

The crowd's idea of justice is fair play between the members of the same class. A sense of honor restrains a gentleman in dealing with gentlemen. Good fellowship forbids taking unfair advantage of one's social comrades. The world, however, will not be redeemed by the club spirit, but by the Christ spirit. The Golden Rule can not be drawn to the scale of any particular class or notion or race. It is that extra margin of justice beyond the crowd's standards which will help to hasten the Kingdom of Heaven. It is in going "the second mile" that we discover the good points of the surly fellow who compelled us to carry his load the first mile. It is in "turning the other cheek" that we feel the adventure of redemption.

The logic of yesterday's course may be projected into a prediction for to-morrow. The Church of Christ must either be distinctive or be damned by disrespect. Our generation will see one of two trends in the Christian enterprise. The church will live more and more at the world's level until ascetic and monastic groups will separate themselves from it in increasing numbers; or the church in a widespread movement will recover the distinctive flavor of holiness that its Master expected of it as "the salt of the earth." May God grant us the wisdom and courage to take the latter, which is the Christlike course.

BELIEF IN CHRIST

In these agitated days to be a heretic is to be a hero, and such a fortune—or fate—has befallen Dr. Fosdick, making him the center of a theological thunder-storm, much to his own regret. Happily, it was a tempest in a tea-pot, since the rumpus ended by inviting the "heretic" to enter the fold in full fellowship. With these things I have not to do, having little interest and no concern, but it is a pity to have so extraordinary a ministry marred, or at least interrupted, by such a debate. Dr. Fosdick was born in Buffalo forty-six years ago, graduated from Colgate University, Union Seminary, and Columbia University, and after nine happy years in the First Baptist Church of Montclair became first an instructor in homiletics and then professor of Practical Theology in Union Seminary; and special preacher at the First Presbyterian Church of New York. His little books for group study, *The Meaning of Prayer, The Meaning of Faith,* and the rest, have had a vast reading in more than one language, while his Cole lectures, *Christianity and Progress,* and his essay on *The Assurance of Immortality,* have helped many a troubled mind. The sermon here given shows a brilliant, driving intellect—I had almost used the word "clever," but that would not be exact—dealing with *Belief* in Christ, not *Faith;* and it reveals the qualities which make him so captivating a preacher to young people—his radiance of personality, his dash and verve of thought, his facility of phrase, his aptness of illustration, his uncanny skill in making an abstruse matter as lucid as light. If one misses the deep, brooding, wooing note, mayhap it will be heard later when time and sorrow make the intellectual difficulties of belief seem like summer manœuvers alongside the tragic warfare of faith with fact.

BELIEF IN CHRIST

HARRY EMERSON FOSDICK, D.D.

FIRST PRESBYTERIAN CHURCH, NEW YORK

"Lord, to whom shall we go? thou hast the words of eternal life. And we have believed and know that thou art the Holy One of God." John 6: 68, 69.

We raised the question last week as to whether it matters that a man believe in God or not. To-day we press a further question: what difference does it make whether or not a man believe in Christ, regard Him as indispensable, and set Him at the center of his thought of God and his interpretation of life? Long ago, as the Fourth Gospel tells us in the sixth chapter, the first disciples faced that question. The crowds that had followed Jesus, disturbed by the loftiness and severity of His demands, were dispersing. "Would ye also go away?" said the Master to the twelve, and Simon Peter gave the answer that has been characteristic of Christianity at its best ever since: "Lord, to whom shall we go? thou hast the words of eternal life. And we have believed and know that thou art the Holy One of God."

83

Does that attitude make any difference? Is Christ indispensable? Is Dr. Burkitt, the Christian scholar, right when he says, "Christianity stands or falls, lives or dies, with the personality of Jesus Christ"? We may well face that question and make our answer as clear and convincing as we can, because to-day many people are disturbed in their estimate of Jesus.

There are no barriers that keep out any questions now, no sacred preserves where people are afraid to push inquiries home. That kind of critical questioning arose with enthusiasm and effect at the time of the Reformation. Folk then asked questions about the church and they were not afraid to push them to radical conclusions. But such critical inquiry could not stop with the church. It turned next to the Bible. People might shrink from investigating the Book, might cry, This is sacred ground and you must keep off! But the answer came back with a will: Nothing that can be thought about is too sacred to be investigated by thought. They searched the Old Testament first, then the New Testament, and, last of all, the life and person and significance of Jesus.

I am sure that this critical questioning is not only necessary to the intellectual integrity of our faith, but that it is salutary. Never fear the consequences in the end. That which is true need not dread investigation. The Bible will emerge at last, seen in a new light, to be sure, reunderstood, reinterpreted, but with its central meanings and messages set free for a larger service than the church has ever known. And Christ can stand investigation—one may be sure of that. Only, while the disturbing process is afoot there are some things we may well take note of. An intelligent Unitarian layman recently said to me with indignation: "Those people are trying to take the halo away from Jesus." Sometimes it does seem so, and if Unitarians may be concerned about it, surely we may be.

Obviously this is true that, so far as organized Christianity is concerned, the personality of Jesus is central. Some of us, for example, deeply desire the progressive unification of Christianity. Christianity does not mean one thing to-day, but many things. It is all split up; it cannot speak with united voice about anything. How many different kinds of folk call themselves Christian! There are Roman Catholics and Protestants a long sea mile apart; high-church Episcopalians and Quakers with a deep gulf between; modernists and fundamentalists with serious divergencies. One wonders sometimes what it is that holds Christianity together anyway.

To be sure, diversity of religious temperament

was in evidence long before the Gospel came. There were literalists leaning for salvation on a text, and mystics feeling religion to be the life of God lived out in the soul of man. There were ecclesiastics thinking of religion in terms of an authoritative organization, and ethicists thinking of religion in terms of a moral and serviceable life. There were individualists valuing chiefly the inward and transforming experiences of the soul, and social reformers valuing religion for its power to remake the world. These differences of religious temperament have not only split up Christianity; they have split up Buddhism in the same way. The sun shines through many panes of colored glass and is changed by each. So has it been with the Gospel. As in Shelley's famous lines:

> Life, like a dome of many-coloured glass,
> Stains the white radiance of Eternity.

Nevertheless, with all these diversities, if you present Christ himself to any Christian, he will kneel. Catholics and Protestants are a long way apart, but when the Catholic sings the praise of Jesus the Protestant sings it too. High-church Episcopalians and Quakers do not speak the same language in religion, but when the Quaker sings Whittier's hymns to Christ the liturgist sings them too. Fundamentalist and modernist do not see eye to eye, but when a modernist sings, "O Master, let me walk with thee," the fundamentalist sings it too. Christ is the magnet that holds this varied mass together. Christ is the mountain down which these divided streams flow. There is one thing we have in common: we all do stand before him and say, "Lord, to whom shall we go? Thou hast the words of eternal life." If anybody is interested then in the unifying of Christianity, Jesus is central. There is only one place where we ever can hope to get Christians together, and that is around Christ.

Again, there are some of us profoundly concerned about the reformation of Christianity. It needs it. To be sure, there are some who still try to think of Christianity as a finished article, its dogmas defined, its duties formulated, its institutions and rituals complete and infallible, a finished article merely to be accepted. But I do not see how they do it. The Gospel of Christ came, an ideal thing, into an unideal world and, in Shakespeare's figure, has been subdued like a dyer's hand to the stuff it works in.

Think what this world would be if all the Christians were really Christian! One-third the population of the planet nominally Christian—what if they were really Christian? Forty million people in the United States nominally Christian—what if they were really Christian? Nobody who cares for mankind's future could pray for a better cause than the reformation of Christianity. But remember this! Whenever in history there has been a real reformation of Christianity, which even for a little while lifted up the church to be a cleansing and transforming force in society, at the heart of it somebody had rediscovered Christ.

It may be Savonarola in the fifteenth century anticipating the Reformation, cleaning up Florence and hurling his challenge at the gross corruption of the church, but you could not listen to him for five minutes in the Duomo without knowing that what had happened to that man was the rediscovery of Christ.

It may be John Wesley, rebelling against the dry-as-dust formalism and dead apathy of English Christianity in his day, leaving behind the stately edifices of the English Church to preach to multitudes on the open hillside, but you could not listen to him, starting that reform whose consequences are not yet done, without seeing that what had happened to him was the rediscovery of Jesus Christ.

When, a few years ago, men like Rauschenbusch called us to a social reformation, reminding us that in our social life we were doing six days in the week things which denied what we said on Sunday, at the center of that movement, the secret of its passion and its power, was the rediscovery of Christ.

Young men who ought to go into the ministry, come, help us to reform Christianity! Only be sure of this: the only kind of reformation that will be real must spring from the rediscovery of the message, meaning, purpose, and spirit of Jesus.

From the standpoint of organized Christianity, therefore, the personality of the Master is central. We never will get Christians together except around Him. We never will reform the church except by the rediscovery of Him. And, one might add, we never will propagate Christianity unless, beyond our theologies and our churches with their western histories and provincialisms, we primarily present him.

There are many of you this morning who will take this centrality of Jesus for granted and gladly will accept those estimates of him in which the historic church has voiced its faith. Very well! Your minds are clear about that. One need not talk to you. But there are others here who will be thinking otherwise.

Let us see if we can state what their thoughts will be. They will be saying that Jesus lived a long time ago, that he was a Jewish teacher sixty generations behind us, who walked in Galilee, and that all this

talk about rediscovering him, organizing people
around him, presenting him, sounds strange.

> Dim tracts of time divide
>   Those golden days from me;
> Thy voice comes strange o'er years of change;
>   How can I follow Thee?
>
> Comes faint and far Thy voice
>   From vales of Galilee;
> Thy vision fades in ancient shades;
>   How should we follow Thee?

And these people will be saying further that Lowell
spoke truth when he remarked that every man is the
prisoner of his date, that is, every man is limited by
the ways of thinking of his generation. So was it
with Jesus, they say. He did not know our modern
science; he had other ways of thinking of the universe, of disease, of the consummation of the age.
If he had not thought the way his generation thought
he never could have been understood by his generation at all. But that fact takes him a long way from
our generation. He does not belong to our time.
How shall we follow him?

And some minds here will go further and say that
those terms which the first century used about Jesus
—"Messiah," that the Jewish Christians employed,
and "Logos," or "Lord," that the Greek Christians

used—were terms perfectly familiar in the first century, but familiar to us no more. They were in existence before Jesus came; they had been used upon other people before they were used on him; and if we are going to have the facts, they say, we must go back behind these categories of understanding, which the first century used and recover in our imagination the individual human figure of the Man of Nazareth. When we do that, they think, we will find an engaging and delightful personality but, after all, a Jewish teacher of the first century concerning whom there is no use fooling ourselves that he is anything more.

I need not tell you such thoughts are going through the minds of this generation, not born of irreverence, but of desire to be honest with the facts. That is what my Unitarian friend meant when he spoke of folks who take the halo from Jesus.

Now, I accept that challenge this morning. I accept it without denying any of these facts we have been rehearsing. Jesus did live a long time ago, and it is amazing that one who lived so long ago should make himself indispensable to our spiritual life. It is true that he thought as his generation thought about many things and could not have been understood by his generation had that not been so. And it is true that if we are to get at the facts we must recover the human figure of the Man of Nazareth. As a teacher in a theological seminary it is my business to know what is being found out about problems like this. But the more I know the more sure I am that in the personality of the Man of Nazareth we are dealing not with a mere Jewish teacher of the first century, but with the transcendent gift of God to the spiritual life of man.

How do we test anything in the long run anyway? Do we not ask what it does, what purposes it serves, what differences it makes to life? What is electricity? I don't know; you don't know; nobody knows. Change the question then. What does electricity do? What are the differences that electricity makes to life? One can grow eloquent about that. Electricity does this and this and this—these manifold and marvelous differences it makes to men. Very well, I answer, then you have discovered something very significant about what electricity is, for electricity must be the kind of force that can do what it does.

Will you approach Christ like that? Who is Christ? You may be puzzled. You may share the uncertainties of your day. You may even fear that time will show that he is just a Jewish teacher of the first century. Very well! Change the question. What has Jesus done? What difference has he made

92

to human life? That is an historic matter. You can
get your hands on that. You can state that. And
as I sketchily state it the recurring theme of our
argument is this: he must be the kind of person
who can do what he has done.

For one thing, he has given man his loftiest idea
of God, not so much by what he said as by what
he was. That is an amazing thing to have done.
In day dreams one may imagine all sorts of wild,
incredible things he might achieve, but one thing I
cannot imagine: that one of us could live a life of
such self-authenticating spiritual grandeur that nineteen centuries from now a man like Browning would
be saying about us:

> The very God! think, Abib; dost thou think?
> So, the All-Great, were the All-Loving too.

I cannot imagine that. Jesus did it. In a world
where multitudes have groped after God, guessed
about God, philosophized about God, he lived a life
of such self-authenticating spiritual grandeur that
increasing multitudes of people when they try to
think about God can say nothing so true, so satisfying, so adequate, as to say that God is like Christ.
That is an amazing thing. He did it. He must have
been the kind of person who could do what he has
done.

Harry Emerson Fosdick, D.D.

Again, he gave the world its loftiest estimate of man. That is an amazing thing too. For it is not easy to hold high estimates of man. There are so many of us—

> The Eternal Saki from that Bowl has poured
> Millions of Bubbles like us, and will pour.

Human life so often, too, is sordid, unlovely, ignoble; we display our low estimates of men in our cruelty to each other in personal relationships, in industry, in war. It is not easy to hold high estimates of man. But Jesus taught that personality in every man or woman, in every king or child, is infinitely precious. And, what is more, he lived as though that were true. He taught men to believe in their divine origin, their spiritual nature, their boundless possibilities. He sent men out saying about themselves what men had never said about themselves before: "Now are we children of God, and it is not yet made manifest what we shall be." That is an amazing thing to have done. Christ's idea of human value haunts us continually. We have tried to work out a little of it in democracy, giving every personality a chance. We have tried to take out of human life sins, like slavery, which desecrate human souls. We hate war because it debauches personality. And in philanthropy we are trying to open doors

94

that handicapped personalities may have a chance. Wherever Jesus goes he lifts immeasurably man's estimate of his own worth. That is a most astonishing thing! He must be the kind of person who could do what he has done.

Once more, the Master has given the world its loftiest ethical ideals. That is strange, because ethical ideals change. They are subject to the flux of time, the alteration of circumstance. As was said long ago, what is right on one side of the Pyrenees is wrong on the other. It is not easy to make a statement about duty in terms of to-day that will hold good a hundred years to come, to say nothing of a thousand. Yet it was not a preacher, it was Glenn Frank, the editor of the *Century Magazine,* who told us the other day that if we Christians would only go back behind our controversies to the ethical teachings of Jesus, we would find something timeless and eternal. As a matter of fact, whenever we do think about what is right, we find Jesus not behind us; he is ahead of us, rallying us, challenging us, alluring us to an adventure toward himself.

And when one thinks of what his teaching has meant to personal character—of all the strong men like Chinese Gordon who wished that they were as strong as Christ; of all the pure women like St. Catherine who wished they were as pure as Christ; of all the adventurous spirits like Livingstone who wished they were as daring as Christ; of all the patient souls like Stevenson who wished they were as patient as Christ; of all the unselfish men like Booth who wished they were as unselfish as Christ —it is amazing! And he must have been the kind of person who could do what he has done.

Again, he not only presented to man his highest ideal, but he supplied power. That is strange. Wherever the Gospel of Jesus has gone, there men have known that they had access into a great resource of spiritual power. At Marston Moor, when the Puritans and the Cavaliers were lining up against each other and the engagement was about to begin, they say that far over the plain the figure of Oliver Cromwell came riding and that at the sight of him the Puritans set up a great, victorious shout as though their battle already had been won. There has been many a battle for goodness on this planet in individual hearts and in social life where the figure of Christ seemed to come up over the horizon and men sent up a triumphant shout as though their battle already had been won. Paul in the first century cried, "I can do all things in him that strengtheneth me." And just this last week, a young Chinese, taking his advanced degree at Columbia, came to make his first public confession of Christ. He is going back to be a superintendent of schools in China, and he said: "I want Christ. I want Christ because I want spiritual power to serve my people in this next generation." Christ has opened innumerable doors to spiritual power. And he must have been the kind of person who could do what he has done.

Once more, as a matter of historical fact, Jesus has given us the transcendent exhibition of trust in spiritual forces. It is not easy for us to trust spiritual forces. We are timid about it. We are like the ancient Sadducee who cried, "My right arm is my god." We understand cynical sayings like "Fortune is always on the side of the largest battalions," or "Trust God, and keep your powder dry." And we smile knowingly when people say that trying to hold humanity together by spiritual forces is like trying to hold the carriages of a railroad train together by relying on the friendly feelings of the engineer for the conductor. It is hard for us to trust spiritual forces. Then Jesus came and did a thing that in range of influence is not simply unique; on a priori grounds it is incredible. It is as though he said, I am going to turn the world upside down; I am going to wield an influence such as no one in history has wielded. Two thousand years from now I am going to hold sway over the imaginations of men and commandeer their allegiance as no emperor nor philosopher has ever done, and I am going to do it by spiritual forces: truth, persuasion, love, and nothing else. I will trust them to the limit, rely on them even though it cost the Cross, and I will win an influence that never has been won before.

I challenge you. Is there any proposition that on a priori grounds is more essentially incredible? And he has done it. It is history now. This next week more millions of knees will bow at the thought of the Cross than ever in history. But that is not all. The most impressive fact is that he is winning us to his principle. We are beginning to see that only as we take our homes from the régime of violence to the régime of spiritual forces have we good homes, that only as we take our schools from the régime of force to the régime of spiritual forces have we right schools; that only as we carry our international relationships out from the domain of force to the governance of spiritual forces can we have a decent world. He is going to win the consent of mankind to his incredible formula. The future belongs to him. Only in spiritual forces is there any hope for the redemption of the world. It is amazing, and he must have been the kind of person who could do what he has done.

We have not touched the garment's hem of what he really did. We have said these things, not because we think them remotely adequate, but because even such a sketchy presentation must make clear that when you go back to that figure in the first century you are not dealing with a diminished rabbi; you are dealing with a transcendent personality, the supreme gift of God to man. Do you really gather up in your imagination what it means to us that he must be the kind of person who could do what he has done—giving the world its loftiest idea of God, its highest estimate of man, its noblest ethical ideals, its deepest spiritual resources, its transcendent exhibition of trust in spiritual power? To be the kind of person who could do that!

I am a liberal. I am not afraid to ask questions about anything. But a personality who is the kind of being that can do that clearly deserves a place at the center of my understanding of God and man. "God was in Christ." What less than that can you say? If you do not find God there, then where will you find him? With Charles Lamb I say that if Shakespeare should come in here now I would stand up; if Christ should come in here I would kneel.

What are you going to do about it? Do you really believe this? Then it means putting Christ at the center of your life. It means taking him in earnest in your private character, in your family, and in all your social relationships. It means saying as Simon

Harry Emerson Fosdick, D.D.

Peter did long ago, turning his back upon every other way of life: "Lord, to whom shall we go? thou hast the words of eternal life. And we have believed and know that thou art the Holy One of God."

THE MOUNTAINS OF GOD

15205

Dr. Gilkey was born in the Old Bay State in 1882, graduated at Harvard University and Union Theological Seminary, with further studies at the Universities of Berlin and Marburg, as well as Free Church College, Glasgow; New College, Edinburgh, and Oxford. He was ordained to the Baptist ministry in 1910, and has since been pastor of the Hyde Park Baptist Church, Chicago: his only parish so far, marked by a distinguished and fruitful ministry. He is a university preacher of unique persuasiveness, having served at Harvard, Yale, Princeton, Cornell, Toronto, Chicago, Stanford, and Purdue. During the past summer he visited India as interpreter, on the Barrows Foundation, of the genius of Christian faith to the men of the East. It was my delight to hear the present sermon on a hot day in July in the Park Avenue Baptist Church, New York, and as a parable of the spiritual life I do not know another like it in our language for its thrill, its challenge, and its wealth of inspiration and suggestion. The reverent attitude of the preacher, his quiet conversational style—like a teacher telling a tale—his evocation of the religious atmosphere, and the eager intentness with which the people listened—it was a scene and a sacrament not to be forgotten. Dr. Gilkey is in the prime and glory of his ministry which, if rich in achievement, is richer still in its promise of wise leadership in the culture of the life of the spirit.

THE MOUNTAINS OF GOD

CHARLES W. GILKEY

HYDE PARK BAPTIST CHURCH, CHICAGO

"Thy lovingkindness, O Jehovah, is in the heavens;
Thy faithfulness reacheth unto the skies.
Thy righteousness is like the mountains of God."
Psalm 36: 5-6. A. R. V.

A few years ago I spent a week in the high Alps, at Wengen in Switzerland, close up under one of the famous mountains of the world. The Jungfrau— great cresting wave of ice and snow forever about to break over the Lauterbrunnen Valley deep below us—dominated our whole life there at Wengen with that silent, mysterious, irresistible authority with which a high mountain always rules the region round it. The very pension in which we lived was called the "Jungfraublick"; and from its garden and windows we could watch the great mountain at all hours and in all weathers. There were rainy days that week when the clouds shut in low-roofed and gray as a flat ceiling; on those days we would never have known that the Jungfrau was there at all, unless we reminded ourselves that it was the power of the mountain which had drawn about her from the blue

Mediterranean a hundred and fifty miles away, the very clouds that hid her from our sight.

There was one day that week never to be forgotten while life lasts: not a cloud in the whole heaven, and every foot of that jagged crest, clear up to the shining summit, sharp and white against the infinite blue. All the incredible glories of a perfect day in the high Alps, from the cold splendors of the sunrise to the warm pink of the evening after-glow, unrolled like a slow panorama of color and majesty before our half-incredulous eyes. It seemed almost too beautiful to be real.

One other day that week, almost as vivid in memory, has since come to be even richer in significance. We had gone for a long walk that afternoon, and seated ourselves presently on one of the benches that the Swiss hotel-keepers provide for their pedestrian guests at commanding points of view. While our backs had been turned to the mountain, a strange thing had happened. A wreath of mist and cloud had gathered just below the summit, exactly as if the maiden for whom the mountain is named had flung about her neck and shoulders a gray scarf of the finest silk. As the eye ran up from the Lauterbrunnen Valley far beneath, across the green fields and darker pines, across the reddish-brown rocks where the grass runs out, and then across the wrinkled, half-dirty glaciers—our view of the mountain stopped short at this silken veil. But higher up, above the cloud, hanging apparently suspended in the sky, shining white with the sun full on it, was something incredibly beautiful to look upon. It might have been a summer afternoon cloud, huge and soft and white in the sunlight, but certain soon to dissolve, or it might be the snowy summit of the Jungfrau. Which was it? For the moment, as we sat there, our eyes could not tell.

As we sat watching that mystery in the sky, it suddenly flashed upon me that there before us in symbol was the characteristic question and perplexity of our half-incredulous modern age about religion. Thoughtful men look up at our Christian faith in a good God Who is our Father, in the immortal life which He has opened before us, in the coming Kingdom of righteousness and peace and joy which is His eternal purpose for His children; and many of them feel about it all very much as we felt looking up at the Jungfrau that afternoon. Religion is certainly very beautiful as it shines there in our human sky, hanging mysteriously between the heaven above us and the earth beneath us, with all the light of our deepest longings and highest aspirations upon it. We should very much like to believe it true. But is it really any more than a summer cloud, born of our traditions and habits and hopes, and reasonably certain to dissolve and disappear when the clear dry light of our modern science and philosophy have worked on it a little longer? Or is it really, as it claims, the summit of all human life and experience, where men may actually meet the Invisible God above them, and become themselves a part of His Eternal Order and Purpose? What is there in religion?

Now it was plainly no original idea of mine that the high mountains could be of some help to us in answering that question. Long centuries ago a Hebrew poet put this same conviction into words far more memorable than any we can find:

> Thy lovingkindness, O Jehovah, is in the heavens;
> Thy faithfulness reacheth unto the skies.
> Thy righteousness is like the mountains of God.

And even more familiar is the somewhat different turn given to a very similar thought in Psalm 125:

> As the mountains are round about Jerusalem,
> So Jehovah is round about his people
> From this time forth and forevermore.

I have wondered often, since that day at Wengen, just what it was that suggested this great comparison to the Psalmist long ago. What is the precise point of similarity between religion in human experience, and the high mountains, that underlies his magnificent figures of speech? Was it the silence that is common to both? Religion at its best never makes a great noise in human life; neither do the mountains. Or was it their mystery? The great experiences and faiths of religion are not by any means always clear even to those who live closest to them; neither are the mountains. Or was it the authority that, in spite of this mystery and silence, gives the mountains so central a place and so mighty an influence in the life of the region and the people round about them? Just such a silent, mysterious, dominating authority has religion always exercised in the lives of men who have once felt its power. Or was it the sense of security, unanalyzed but pervasive and controlling, that, as the Psalmist explicitly reminds us, steadies and reassures the mountain-dweller and the religious man alike?

Whatever the insight that first prompted this comparison, it has not been limited to religious thinkers and poets of long ago. When I was a student in Germany in 1909, I came across a German translation of an anonymous article entitled "Credo," that had appeared in the *Hibbert Journal* for April of that year. I was so impressed by the translation that I hunted up the English original and copied two

or three sentences from it upon a card which I still
have, faded and soiled with much loaning and re-
peated reference. It has since transpired that the
author was the editor himself, Principal L. P. Jacks
of Manchester College, Oxford, for whose thoughts
on religion the whole western world has learned to
listen. Here are the memorable sentences upon the
card:

> Religion therefore does not apologize for itself, does not
> stand on the defensive, does not justify its presence in the
> world. If theorists would vindicate Religion, they may do so:
> but Religion comes forth in the majesty of silence, like a
> mountain amid the lifting mists. All the strong things of the
> world are its children; and whatever strength is summoned to
> its support is the strength which its own spirit has called into
> being.

We have good precedent, therefore, both ancient
and modern, both Scriptural and literary, for asking
the mountains to help us answer this prevalent and
characteristic question of our modern age: what is
there in religion, or to it?

I

There is *reality* in religion. Of course there are
hundreds of American tourists who on some hurried
travel-bureau schedule go up from Visp to Zermatt
hoping for a glimpse of the Matterhorn. All their

lives they have seen pictures—keep one hanging in their home perhaps—of that gigantic forefinger of rock with its nail of ice, pointing up into the open heaven. It has been one of the ambitions of their European trip to see the Matterhorn for themselves. But as they leave the train, the clouds are hanging thick over Zermatt, and drifting in wisps among the pine trees close at hand. No Matterhorn anywhere to be seen! And all day long, as they sit anxious and eager on the hotel veranda, or wander up and down the narrow village street, there is never a glimpse of the mountain, and only guesses from pictures and conversation as to where it stands hidden from their sight. The inexorable necessities of an American sight-seeing schedule that whirls them through Europe largely on "one-night stands," drag them sorely disappointed to the train down the steep valley again. Have they seen the Matterhorn? No. But would they be foolish enough to tell their friends at home that, having been to Zermatt for themselves and seen nothing worth while, they have concluded that there is no real basis for all this talk about the Matterhorn?

Yet otherwise sensible people are continually making a similar snap-judgment about religion. They happen into church some Sunday morning just to see what it is like, and find the sermon dull—as it doubtless frequently is—and the service uninterest-ing—as it must be where there is no spontaneous spirit of worship to quicken it into life. Or they drop a remark or raise a question to some religiously minded friend, but the ensuing conversation does not find a real trail that leads anywhere. Quite as often perhaps there is no pretense of or interest in any personal verification. On the slender basis of some such hasty glimpse or complacent indifference, rests the cocksure comment: "Religion? Nothing to it."

The reality of religion vindicates itself, mysterious and obscure as it often seems at first sight, by three tests strikingly similar to those by which the moun-tain evidences itself as real. In both cases it is constantly necessary, first, to check present perplex-ities by past experiences. What finally assured us that afternoon on the Swiss bench that the shining something we saw in the sky was not a summer cloud soon to dissolve, but the mountain's solid summit? Not so much our doubtful eyes, as our vivid memo-ries. The day of the long walk to the bench came after the cloudless day, when the outline of the suc-cessive crests of the Monch and the Eiger and the Jungfrau had fixed itself so sharply upon my memory that to this day I can shut my eyes and see that magnificent sky-line. And as on the bench that afternoon I compared that vivid memory with the upper edge of the enigma in the sky, I became slowly sure that it was no summer cloud, but the mountain itself.

Now there are great moments of insight in religious experience, comparable to that perfect day in the mountains. They may be as rare in a lifetime as such days are in some Alpine summers; but when they do come, they are no less real and revealing. They show us where the heights really lie, and which are highest. Religion has its own distinctive names for these unusual experiences: the older phraseology called them conversion, regeneration, sanctification, the second blessing, the baptism of the Spirit; the newer vocabulary speaks of insight, exaltation, mystic union, communion with God. Whatever the terms we use, the common fact of spiritual experience is that most of us have to orient our lives through many dull and even dark days, by what we can see clearly only now and then. As Matthew Arnold puts it:

> Thy tasks in hours of insight willed
> May be in hours of gloom fulfilled.

But there are many folk to whom these hours of clear religious insight seem not to come—or at least seem to have stopped coming. They hear others tell of their conversion, or of some deep mystical

111

experience in worship or prayer; and complain in all sincerity that they do not understand what it is all about. There remains for them a second test, by which the Jungfrau also evidences herself through the considerable periods when clear days do not come. The Swiss mountaineer can tell us best what this test is. If he were to add up in parallel columns for any month, or at least for any year, the number of days when he sees the high mountains and those when he does not, there would doubtless often be more in the second column than in the first. But though he may not see the mountain half the time, it is constantly proving itself a dominating fact at a dozen important points in his daily experience. Its influence is woven into the very texture of his living. The mountain makes his climate, summoning and precipitating the snow and rain that water his garden and provide pasture for his flocks. The fame and beauty of the mountain attract visitors from all over the world, who insure the economic prosperity of his little valley. More than that, the mountain molds his character. The historic "Cradle of Liberty" is not so truly, as we provincial New Englanders suppose, in Faneuil Hall in Boston, as it is in those Swiss mountain valleys where since the Middle Ages fathers and sons have loved their freedom, and fought and died to maintain it. The Swiss

112

mountaineer is chiefly sure of the mountain because he lives with it, and finds it a dependable and dominating factor in his daily experience.

Just so, in spite of all the mysteries and obscurities which we cannot completely escape or explain, is it with religion. Its best evidence is the stimulating and molding influence which it can and does bring to bear throughout the whole range of higher human living. It becomes the central and dominating fact of life to those who really live with it; who, in the language of the Psalms, "abide under the shadow of the Almighty."

One other test remains, for those who have the patience and determination to apply it. A man may climb the mountain for himself, and, standing upon its topmost summit, look out upon the world below with that exaltation and exultation which only the man who stood there ever knows. Just so a man may experience religion in some such conclusive fashion as shall give him the personal assurance of the climber who has himself "been up there." But, if one is to apply that decisive test of personal experience in either realm, there are some necessary conditions which must first be met. Men do not achieve any of the heights of life without prolonged previous self-discipline. Weak muscles and weak wills must first be hardened by patient training in

self-mastery. The heart must be strengthened till
it can bear its unusual burden upward step by step,
in spite of the rarer air, all the way to the summit.
The head must be steadied until it can look far down
without dizziness and far up without discouragement
—a steadiness which as Jesus warned us is not easily
achieved in things spiritual, where most of us fall
victims to pride the moment we climb a little way
above our fellows, or to lack of faith when we look
up toward God. Nor is this preparatory period of
training either easy or short.

> Let no man think that sudden in a minute
>   All is accomplished and the work is done;—
> Though with thine earliest dawn thou shouldst begin it
>   Scarce were it ended in thy setting sun.

But to him who will meet these inexorable conditions, the heights of life are accessible on the same
terms as the summits of the Alps.

While we are thinking of reality in religion, one
other point is not without present-day significance.
Suppose a geological expedition were to examine some
side valley or shoulder of the mountain and after
careful research with the best technique and highest
scholarship available should come back to report that
the geological structure and history of that region
were somewhat different from what had previously

been supposed. We should all agree that our geological theories and text-books must be revised to accord with this new knowledge—but we should never fear that anything serious had happened, or could happen, to the mountain itself. Scientific expeditions will come and go over the mountain for centuries to come, and will revise and correct their text-books and their theories times without number; but the mountain itself will outlast them all, summoning its storms and calling its lovers and supporting the dwellers in its shadow, down through the generations. Just so is it in religious history and experience. Improved scholarship will doubtless continue for centuries to come, as for decades past, to make new discoveries about the authorship of the Pentateuch and the Psalms and the prophets, the history of Christianity and of other religions, the psychological processes of religious experience, the evolution of life upon this planet; and these discoveries may require the frequent revision of our theological text-books and theories. But meanwhile religion itself will continue to grip and bless and sustain the hearts of men, pointing and lifting them up toward God and duty and immortality, with solid ground beneath their feet as they climb. The mountain itself standeth sure, however men's theories about it may change.

Charles W. Gilkey

Lord, thou hast been our dwelling-place
In all generations.
Before the mountains were brought forth,
Or ever thou hadst formed the earth and the world,
Even from everlasting to everlasting, thou art God.

II

But, further, there is *power* in religion. That
summer in Switzerland the railway stations were
placarded with picturesque posters, inviting the Swiss
people to subscribe their savings toward a bond issue
to complete the electrification of the railroads. They
are in part electrified already. On the ride up the
steep valley from Visp to Zermatt to see the Matterhorn, the train slips into motion without a jerk
and slides up the stiffest grades apparently with
almost as much ease as it would coast down. The
power that drives that train, and scores of others at
the same time, is "white coal," brought not from a
mine but from a dynamo. The dynamo is driven
by a mountain stream. The stream gets its energy
from the mountain's height, and is itself made up
from a thousand trickling rivulets fed by the slow
glaciers and the eternal snows. And these in their
turn are born in a process over which nature always
throws a veil of impenetrable cloud. When it rains
or snows on the mountains, we in the valleys be-

116

low can see the results, but never the process itself. Any one who starts out to investigate that process soon discovers how very easy it is to lose one's way in the veil of mystery that always surrounds it. All that we can see from the valleys is that next morning, when the clouds have cleared, the summits are shining white with new-fallen snow, and all the streams are brimming with fresh energy. Just so is it with men's communion with God in worship and in prayer. The results are plain to see, even though the process is obscure to trace. So Jesus hinted when he said: "But thou, when thou prayest, enter into thy closet, and, when thou hast shut thy door, pray to thy Father which is in secret; and thy Father, which seeth in secret, shall reward thee openly."

> As torrents in summer,
> Half dried in their channels,
> Suddenly rise, though the
> Sky is still cloudless,
> For rain has been falling
> Far off at their fountains,
>
> So hearts that are fainting
> Grow full to o'erflowing,
> And they that behold it
> Marvel and know not
> That God at their fountains
> Far off has been raining.

Charles W. Gilkey

In a sermon that I heard twenty years ago as an undergraduate, that thinker-poet among great American preachers, Dr. George A. Gordon of Boston, pointed out that high mountain ranges may be profitably studied from various and complementary points of view. The geologist, the botanist, the biologist, the sociologist, the historian, will all find rewarding fields for research in the Alps or the Himalayas. But not the least significant aspect of the mountains is their strange power over the invisible air above them, out of which they draw down the snow and rain that bring fertility and potential energy to all the region round. So is it also, he said, of human nature. We may profitably study the processes of its development, the influence of its environment, the history of its achievements. But not the least significant of its aspects is its strange power over the Invisible above it; its religious capacity to draw down blessing from its contact and communion with the Unseen.

And he might have gone on to point out, as Dr. Henry S. Coffin has done so vividly in his latest book, that the spiritual power thus generated in personal religious experience, manifests and applies itself over all the broad areas of human life. The same stream that drives the Swiss dynamos rushes on into the valley to water the gardens and wash

the stained garments of the peasants who live there;
further still, it supports and makes possible the stren-
uous progress of the swimmer from bank to bank;
lower yet, flowing into the Rhine or the Rhone, it
bears up the heavily laden barges of a national and
international commerce; and if the returning American traveler chance to embark at Rotterdam, his
ocean liner will steer out into the sunset on the
broad bosom of that same widening stream. So the
spiritual energy that is created when men meet with
God in public worship and in private prayer, flows
down across all the continent of human life, bringing power for their tasks, fertility and beauty to
their gardens, forgiveness and cleansing for their sins,
and support for their heaviest burdens. And when
at last we too are homeward bound, out of the river
toward the ocean and the sunset, religion bears us
up in faith and immortal hope on our voyage over
strange seas to the Other Shore.

III

One other thing there is in religion, the right word
for which is not easy to find. It often begins as
adventure. Some of us are so constituted that in the
mountains we cannot be satisfied to sit too long upon
the hotel veranda, or even to loiter along the village

street; Alpenstock in hand and Rucksack on our backs, we too must be up and climbing. The spell of the mountains is on us, and will not let us go. But when our daily climbs have taken us up to the higher ranges where the trees and grass run out, the patches of snow begin, the brooks trickle white from under the glaciers, and the nearer summits beckon close at hand, then adventure becomes *discovery*. That is the only word for it, when one looks down from some superb prospect upon the huddled houses and the crawling train in the valley far below, and then again up, above the winding glaciers all around, to the snow-crowned summits beyond. It is all a new world. But I notice that a friend of mine who once climbed the Matterhorn always uses still another word when he describes his experience on that summit. He calls it a *revelation*.

So there are some men who begin the religious quest as an heroic adventure of human spirit when it is restless and dissatisfied in the comfortable valleys of life, and eager to attempt its higher ranges. But what started as a spiritual adventure becomes then the discovery of a new world around and beyond them, whose wonder they never guessed from the valleys below, and whose power over and within them grows with every experience of it. At first they had thought it was only their own aspiration that urged them upward; but later they found a world of realities around and above them as they climbed, which those never discover who are content to remain always in the valley. Then it appeared that the urge within, which had kept them climbing, was the strengthening response of their own souls to this new world of truth and beauty and goodness which is God's own country. And when there they meet with Him, and in His presence look out upon life as He sees it—the word which religion has always used for that ultimate experience is not simply adventure and aspiration, nor even discovery, but revelation.

These heights most men do not attain by themselves alone—nor yet without a guide. They told us in Zermatt that all the serious accidents thereabouts for many years had befallen those who were foolish enough to risk high climbing alone, or in a company of amateurs without an experienced guide. It is not done that way in the mountains—or in religion. We rope ourselves together in the spiritual fellowship of a church, or at the very least in the company of others like-minded, in order that if any slip, he may not utterly fall. And when we find a guide who knows the way to the summit, we follow him implicitly.

In the main street of Chamonix, under the very

shadow of Mont Blanc, stands a monument commemorative of the first ascent of the mountain in 1787. The figure of the Genevan naturalist, De Saussure, is standing erect, looking up at the mountain itself; and one look at his face tells the visitor what is in his heart. Beside him, bent over with eagerness, one hand pointing the way up, is the guide, Jacques Balmat, who in the previous year had made his way to the summit. One who tarries a little beneath the monument can almost hear the guide saying to the other, as he stands there gripped by the grandeur and the challenge of the monarch of the Alps: "Come. I've been up there. I know the way. Follow me, and we'll go up together."

Just so Jesus Christ comes to each one of us, as we catch sight of the heights of life, the presence of God, the world unseen and eternal; and feel in our deepest souls their challenge and claim upon us. His hand rests in comradeship and encouragement upon our shoulder; His outstretched arm points out the climbing path ahead; His voice speaks, quiet but confident, in our ear. "Come. I've been there. I know the way. Follow me, and we will go together."

THE OLD-TIME RELIGION

Born in Pittsburgh thirty-nine years ago, Dr. Luccock was educated at Northwestern University and Union Seminary and entered the Methodist ministry in 1910. After two pastorates in Connecticut he became instructor in the New Testament in Drew Theological Seminary, and, later, Editorial Secretary of the Methodist Board of Foreign Missions. At the last General Conference Dr. Luccock was made contributing editor to all the leading journals of the Methodist Church. Among his earlier writings are *Fares, Please* and *Skylines,* brief, vivid, sparkling essays uniting human passion and spiritual insight with delicious humor and a unique gift of putting old truths as if they were new discoveries. His recently published book of sermons, *The Haunted House,* took everybody captive, as witness the verdict of a keen appraiser:

"Right in our own day a new sort of sermon has been evolved. This new sermon is written by a man of letters who reads everything and lets every characteristic aspect of American life blow through his mind as the winds blow through the leaves of the trees. Then he brings all this knowledge and feeling to the test of the great experiences and expressions of the Old and New Testaments. The contrast is something electric. William James jostles Jeremiah, and James Robinson is found in the company of the Apostle Paul. Neither Christopher Morley nor Don Marquis has a more intimate contact with all that is going on in the big towns of to-day. And no paragraph writer has a surer command of speech which leaves burrs sticking in the mind than has Dr. Luccock. But all this sensitive apprehension of the waves of feeling which run through the life of our people, all this capacity to find the arresting word and the cohesive phrase, are brought to the service of a Christian interpretation of the problems which beset men to-day. You feel as if preaching is a new and fresh adventure."

THE OLD-TIME RELIGION [1]

HALFORD E. LUCCOCK, D.D.

EDITORIAL SECRETARY, METHODIST BOARD OF FOREIGN MISSIONS

"By faith Abraham went forth, although he did not know where he was to go." Hebrews 11: 8.
"Let my people go!" Exodus 5: 1.

The principal trouble with "the old-time religion," as that phrase is frequently understood, is that it is not *old enough!* We are all familiar with the song, usually pealed out in lusty tones:

> Give to me the old-time religion,
> It's good enough for me!
> It was good enough for Moses,
> It was good enough for father,
> It was good enough for mother,
> And it's good enough for me!

What a man who sings that song is clamoring for, when it is anything more than an emotional outlet, is not nearly so old as he thinks it is. He is usually thinking of the exact form of religious expression and

[1] From *The Haunted House and Other Sermons.* Copyrighted 1923, by Halford E. Luccock. Used by courtesy of The Abingdon Press, Inc.

125

practice familiar to him as a boy. And that is a very modern invention, comparatively speaking.

The particular combination of ideas and customs which is dignified by the title of "old-time religion" is frequently like one of the modern spurious paintings passed off on the uninitiated as an "old master." It is not a genuine "antique," which dates back to the creative days of the faith, but a local version which flourished about 1850, or at best in the middle of the seventeenth century. This whole sermon can be put into one sentence: If you want the "old-time religion"—and nothing is so desperately needed by the world to-day—be sure you get it *old enough.* Do not run back into the sixteenth century and stop there. Insist on the real thing. Go clear back to the beginning.

Notice swiftly three things about the frequent longing for "the old-time religion" with its inevitable implied disparagement of the Christian faith of the present day.

First, the sighing for the religion of yesterday is a *delusion.* Of course religion ought to be old. It can't be worth much if it is not. The sun which lights the earth was not made yesterday. The hills which give birth to the streams which water the earth are not a twentieth-century product. When we wish to mark a thing as being really old we can say noth-

126

ing so strong as that it is as "old as the hills." A religion to be worth anything must be so old as to be timeless. This truth is expressed in one of the most picturesque and suggestive titles of God in the Old Testament, "The Ancient of Days." It is only when we can say, "Lord, thou hast been our dwelling place in all generations," that we feel the lifting power of faith.

But while all that is eternally true usually the cry for the old-time religion is not a thirsting for the universal, timeless elements of religion—those large aspects of Christian truth which are the same yesterday, to-day, and forever. It is, rather, for those local and temporary forms which have become stereotypes of the mind. And the paradoxical thing about it is that those particular interpretations which are revered as being old are comparative novelties. The rampant fundamentalist, for instance, seeking whom he may devour, who regards any interpretation of Christ more liberal than his own as one of Satan's masterpieces, is not merely so much concerned over the triumph of the Spirit of Christ, as over his success in ramming his own dogma down people's throats. He labels as "the old-time religion" a belief in the verbal inspiration of the Scriptures. That particular belief is really quite a new-fangled idea, as any student of the history of Scripture knows.

Halford E. Luccock, D.D.

Many, if not most, of those who declare that the old-time religion, which was good enough for Moses, for father, for mother, and for Shadrach, Meshach, and Abednego, and is consequently good enough for them, identify it with the theological interpretations and even with the science (there lies the rub!) held in certain localities two generations ago. Their attitude of mind is exactly like that of the old lady who bitterly opposed the stained-glass windows in the new church, saying that she preferred the glass "just as God made it." Both glass and theology are made out of elements supplied by God. But neither comes directly from the hand of the Almighty.

This vociferous cry for the old-time religion is an *evasion*. The chorus, "Give me the old-time religion," is one in which many join. The big business man, in disgust and despair over an impertinent, unobsequious, social type of religion which comes into his office and asks, "What percent do you make on your investments?"—"How much of your stock is watered?"—"How much do you pay your employees?" cries passionately, "Give me the old-time religion!" It was much easier to get along with. As long as he subscribed to the fund for the relief of worn-out preachers, it did not interfere very much with his business. To-day many business men's associations are trying to say with a boycott on those organizations which dare to advocate putting Christianity into practice, "The old-time religion is good enough for me!"

To the man looking out on a perplexing world with its new scientific understanding and social emphasis, the simple, individualistic, emotional religion of two generations ago was ever so much easier to get adjusted to. Earth is so much more bothersome than heaven! So the man who does not like to mix thought with his religion looks back longingly to the days when it was considered sufficient merely to sing about it.

The unintelligent sigh for yesterday's religion is *a repression of to-day's new insight*. It says lazily, "The old is better." Back to grandfather's world and to grandmother's Bible! Such a blind appeal to the near past and the local past strangles every new birth of conscience. Nothing could be more destructive of a genuine and creative faith than to model manners and morals and convictions by the standards of yesterday. Some one has said regarding Southern novels that too many Southern authors squatted about in military cemeteries to write their books. A good many religious books have been written in military cemeteries! Their chief themes are

> Old, unhappy, far-off things
> And battles long ago.

129

Halford E. Luccock, D.D.

When we stay in the cemetery too long we catch a cold and *rigor mortis* sets in. It has been well pointed out by George Adam Smith that the kingdom of God is not obstructed by being blown up, but by being sat upon. The most effective way of sitting upon the kingdom of God to-day is to begin to sing about the old-time religion.

The emphasis so far has been negative. But I would like to make one as emphatically positive as I may and plead for the old-time religion as earnestly as any camp meeting exhorter might. My only concern is that it be the genuine article!

Leap the centuries and you will find two things.

I

The old-time religion is the religion of Abraham —a religion of intellectual and spiritual daring. The "old-time religion" of his day was not good enough for Abraham. Not by a thousand miles! He traveled that far to Canaan to find one good enough. The religion which really is old is not a mechanical perpetuation of the dead forms of other days. It is pioneering for God into new fields and new days. Abraham went forth although he did not know where he was to go. Had he followed the practice of many to-day, he would have answered God's call to venture

130

forth by a timorous "No, thank you. Ur suits me all right. The old-time religion is good enough for me!"

He walked west with God, even when that daring exploit took him directly in the face of every time-honored and revered orthodoxy of his neighbors.

What a venture it was! Professor F. H. Giddings asks an unusual but fascinating question, "Why was there ever any history at all?" It is well worth thinking about. Why did anything ever happen that made events to be recorded? Why was not the record of the race simply one long afternoon of cattle grazing, in which all history could be summed up in one inglorious word—"ditto"? The answer is that history was made by the adventurers. The Order of the Sons of Abraham created history. They have made the history of religion, beginning with Abraham and going on up through the prophets, on and up until there comes that utterly reckless Innovator, Jesus of Nazareth, who announces in a perfectly scandalous way, "Ye have heard it said of old, . . . but I say unto you." Any future history of Christianity worth recording will come from the same source—from men daring enough to push out into the world of thought and life, to adapt Christianity to the needs and temper of their time, men who dare to strip the husk from the kernel of truth and separate the accidental from the essential.

Halford E. Luccock, D.D.

General Smuts, in that noble figure of speech derived from Abraham himself, said, "Humanity has struck its tents and is on the march." It is a tragedy if the church is left behind in a walled city. Oh, for a baptism of that old-time religion of Abraham! Will Christianity go before this moving column of men as a pillar of fire, or will it be left behind like a collection of pyramids in ancient Egypt, dedicated to the past, peopled by mummies? Will the church have intellectual daring enough to make itself and its message at home in the new intellectual world we live in? Will it have the spiritual daring of Abraham to respond to the call of God which comes through the needs of the world to-day, "Get thee out"? Get thee out of the familiar and comfortable ruts of custom, out of the smug little dogmatisms which make void the Word of God through the accumulated tradition of unessential trifles! Get thee out of the world of petty ecclesiastical red tape and into the promised land of great fundamental human needs! Maude Royden has graphically pictured the failure of negative, conventional traditions to meet deep human needs when she tells of a friend of hers who was hungering for some explanation of the meaning of pain and sorrow, and who went to the church only to be told that one must not marry his deceased wife's sister! Since the war in America there has been a widespread theological reaction depressing in the extreme. An ignorant obscurantism, the deadliest enemy which Christianity faces, is trying to identify Christianity in the minds of millions of people with adherence to wholly impossible and grotesque views of science and history. This, of course, is only a temporary backwash of the war. Already signs appear that it has reached the ebb tide, just as the other reactions due to the war in economics and politics are being exhausted. An overdose of "normalcy" is turning bitter in the mouth.

Let us bring that question back to the individual. Can we ourselves keep step with Abraham? Have we the "old-time religion" which can cling to the great realities of the spiritual life and leave unessential and irrelevant things behind, as Abraham left the traditions of Ur? It is only as we commend our faith to the mind of the time that we can ever hope to have it command the time.

Abraham Lincoln has left the church a noble watchword:

The dogmas of the quiet past are inadequate to the stormy present. The occasion is piled high with difficulty and we must rise to the occasion. As our case is new, so must we think anew and act anew. We must disenthrall ourselves and then we shall save our country.

133

Halford E. Luccock, D.D.

Consider two concrete examples. There is no realm where this daring is so needed as in *the crusade against war*. One would think that the whole force of the church would be violently thrown against war. But actually nothing of the kind has taken place. There are a thousand resolutions passed, a million Christmas sermons on the Prince of Peace, but to take a positive stand against war—all war— still demands the spirit and daring of a martyr. It is easy to be against war until a tense situation arises. Then the spirit of nationalism throttles the spirit of Christ. There is no hope for the world unless the Church of Christ sets its face against war like a flint and is willing to sacrifice daringly for the goal of a warless world. It has been well suggested that we ought to add one more commandment to our Decalogue, "Thou shalt not make the next war holy."

In the realm of church unity the definite call comes to get out of the old habitations into the Promised Land. Can we move out of our isolated and complacent sectarianism into genuine working federation? There is little hope of the church exerting any commanding influence in national life when it asks the world to listen to the clamorous disputes of a debating society, instead of to the voice of the Christian Church. "What army," asks Macaulay, "com-

manded by a debating society every achieved anything but disgrace?" We have finally learned how
unity of command on the Western Front during the
war was brought about. It was not by any far-
visioned strategy of the leaders, nor by any broad
wisdom of the government. It was brought about by
only one thing—the drive of Hindenburg's army in
the spring of 1918, which threatened to end the war
any day with a German victory. That gigantic and
perilous onslaught did what nothing else could do—
it swept away national jealousies and welded all the
fighting forces into one single swinging sword. Perhaps that is just what is happening to the church
before our eyes. Perhaps we ought to be down on
our knees thanking God for the desperate situation
of the world to-day if that situation actually brings
the working unity of all the soldiers of Christ.

II

*The old-time religion was the religion of Moses—
a religion of social revolution.* Perhaps "revolution"
is a strong word. So be it. The religion of Moses
was a strong thing. It was a blazing conviction which
thundered at the established order in Egypt, in behalf of the depressed, defrauded, exploited people,
the command, "Let my people go!" The familiar

135

hymn of praise to the old-time religion has one line which declares, "It was good enough for Moses." That is an unmitigated slander. After his vision of God in the desert Moses was not content with any worn conventionalities. He had learned that the will of God meant the release of the toilers, the bondsmen. The social gospel is not any new thing. It is one of the oldest things in the Bible. It was one of the first results of the vision of God which came to Moses. And any religion which does not have that social vision and throbbing sympathy for men at its very center can have any claim to being an old-time religion. It is a pale, bloodless modern substitute.

"Give me the old-time religion!" Let the world hear from millions of Christian voices the echoes of the command of God, "Let my people go." Let it reverberate through the United States, now left without adequate protection for its children against the exploitation of those who profit by child labor. Let it sound like the crack of doom thundering in the ears of Pharaoh in those States where children under fourteen years of age are forced to labor for ten to twelve hours a day under the shameful permission of the State. I believe that adequate protection requires a federal amendment prohibiting child labor. We are told by lawyers that we ought not to "clutter up the Constitution" with amendments. But let us repeat in high seriousness a remark first made in jest, "What's the Constitution between friends?" What is the Constitution between God and his friends, the children? I would much rather see the Constitution cluttered up with a dozen more amendments than to see the nation cluttered up with a million undersized, malformed children deprived of their birthright!

In the whole world of industry we need the old-time religion which undertakes to transform an iniquitous economic order. One of the largest textile mills of New England was closed down for months by a strike which was brought about by its announced intention of reducing wages. The plea of the company was that it would not be possible to continue to pay the wages and stay in business. Yet all the time during the strike it has been paying on its stock thirty and forty percent. How long will we continue to allow such industrial housekeeping to go on?

We must dare to attack the king of the industrial order. The king in his purple robes on the throne is the profit motive. Society is organized around the wrong center—on the motive of acquisition. The only remedy that will treat society's sickness is to organize it around the motive of service. And the

Halford E. Luccock, D.D.

first step, though not by any means the only one, but one in which we can all do something immediate, is to show the world a group of men and women who are redeemed from the domination of the profit motive in their own lives.

So we have arrived at the end—where every sermon should find its journey's end—at the feet of Jesus. The old-time religion is the religion of Jesus —a religion of active, sacrificing love.

The Rev. G. A. Studdert Kennedy has well caught the spirit of that eternal appeal of Jesus:

> Passionately fierce the voice of God is pleading,
>   Pleading with men to arm them for the fight.
> See how those hands, majestically bleeding,
>   Call us to rout the armies of the night.
> Not to the work of sordid, selfish saving
>   Of our own souls to dwell with him on high;
> But to the soldier's splendid selfless braving
>   Eager to fight for righteousness and die.
> Bread of thy body give me for my fighting,
>   Give me to drink thy sacred blood for wine,
> While there are wrongs that need me for the righting,
>   While there is warfare splendid and divine.[1]

[1] From *Poems*, by G. A. Studdert Kennedy. Reprinted by permission George H. Doran Company.

THE BLEEDING VINE

Dr. Hillis has had an extraordinary career as preacher and publicist: the facts of his life are almost too familiar to be recited, his qualities too well known to need appraisal. Born in Iowa sixty-seven years ago, educated at Lake Forest University and McCormick Theological Seminary, after pastorates at Peoria and Evanston, he succeeded to the pulpit of Central Church, Chicago: an independent church founded and made famous by David Swing—a teacher from whom he had learned much, both in literary habit and in the art of making essay-sermons. His ministry in Chicago was a dazzling triumph, made so by the fascination of his personality, his journalistic instinct, his incredible fertility of thought and felicity of style. His earliest books, *The Investment of Influence* and *A Man's Value to Society,* sold almost like novels; and his *Great Books as Life Teachers* fixed, if it did not introduce, the "book-sermon" in American preaching. After four years in Chicago he followed Dr. Lyman Abbott in Plymouth Church, Brooklyn— the church glorified by the genius of Beecher. Again it was a triumph, albeit by a different method, becoming less an essayist and more a preacher: perhaps the greatest master of popular homiletics in his generation. For almost thirty years he has published a sermon every week, an amazing feat, requiring a richness of resource well-nigh unbelievable. Books flashed from his pen, like sparks from the anvil of a busy smithy, essays, lectures, and at least one novel; but perhaps *The Influence of Christ in Modern Life,* though not so widely known, will be longest remembered. In his last book, *The Great Refusal,* he is not only a preacher, but an evangelist, using his rich gifts and ripened powers to induce youth to burn its bridges and to swear instant fidelity to the convictions of the Christian religion.

THE BLEEDING VINE [1]

NEWELL DWIGHT HILLIS, D.D.

PLYMOUTH CHURCH, BROOKLYN

"And, behold, a woman in the city, which was a sinner, when she knew that Jesus sat at meat in the Pharisee's house, brought an alabaster box of ointment, and stood at his feet behind him, weeping and began to wash his feet with tears, and did wipe them with the hairs of her head, and kissed his feet and anointed them with the ointment. . . . And he said to the woman, Thy faith hath saved thee; go in peace." Luke 7: 38, 39, 50.

As an apology for the slenderness of his book of reminiscences, the Beloved Disciple, with oriental imagery, said, if all the deeds and words of Jesus had been preserved the whole world could not contain the books that would be written. John means that if one sermon on the Mount was recorded, hundreds were never reported; that if a few brilliant parables, like the story of the Lost Coin, the Lost Sheep, and the Lost Son, were written out, thousands of parables existed only in the memory of the eager hearers; and that if some wonder deeds of mercy were de-

[1] From *The Great Refusal*, by Dr. Hillis. Used by courtesy of F. H. Revell Co.

141

scribed in the Memorabilia of the Master, that other thousands were known only to the recipients of His kindness. But it could not have been otherwise. Consider the fertility of the intellect of Jesus! His mind blazed like a star, glowing and sparkling with ten thousand brilliant effects.

His genius was a rich garden, putting forth fruit and flowers in every nook and corner, and no hand could do more than pluck a few blossoms here and there. In August the whole land waves with leaves and flowers from Maine to Oregon. Then winter comes, invading the vineyards and harvest fields. Always the north wind leads the armies of destruction. Fierce gales flail the boughs of maple and whip the branches, and the leaves fall in millions. When December comes the forests are bare save where, here and there, the oak leaves adhere to their boughs, like fragile bronze. Now and then a botanist, chilled by the snow, refreshes his memory by looking at the leaves he pressed and the flowers he placed between the pages of his notebook, but it is a far cry from a pressed violet and rose to June bloom and universal summer. These slender reminiscences of Luke's Master represent a few pressed flowers plucked in the garden of his memory. The hand of Luke was made for one golden bough and not for all beautiful forests. In trying to interpret that myriad-minded Master and His efflorescent genius, we must pass from this handful of incidents, this score of parables, to the rich gardens where these flowers were plucked and to the veins of silver and of gold from which this treasure was taken by loving hands. The artist may paint a few canvases, but no painter will ever be a historian of the full summer. The limitations of the human intellect make it certain that the life of Christ will never be written.

Why, then, did Luke and John pass by ninety-nine incidents, and record this particular one? Man's first duty is to discover himself, who he is, where he came from, what he is here for and whither he is going. But there is a larger task and a higher knowledge. "Let not the wise man glory in his wisdom, nor the strong man in his strength, nor the rich man in his gold, but let him glory in this, that he understandeth and knoweth God." That which storms can never reveal, that which earthquakes can never proclaim, must be found out by the soul. Every man paints his own portrait of God, but the heart and not·the intellect is the artist that limns the canvas. The supreme question is, "How does the Unseen Being feel toward His children, in the hour of their sorrow, suffering, or moral disaster?" In the belief that what Jesus was during three years in Palestine, the all-helpful God is in all ages and lands, the biographers of Jesus selected out of thousands of incidents those episodes that would portray the heart of God, the gentleness of His strength, the mercy of His justice, and the tenderness of His verdict upon the career of His children. They passed by the omniscience of God, the wisdom of Jesus, His regency over physical nature, and taking men at the point where the heart is broken and the steps have wandered, they set forth the way that Jesus bore Himself toward the poor pilgrims, lying like bleeding vines torn from the wall, like the snowdrops and anemone, trampled into the ground by the feet of the multitude.

It is not an accident, therefore, that all four of the biographers of Jesus have told in detail the story of the feast in the home of Simon. Luke alone remembers the parable of the Prodigal Son; Matthew recalls the very words of the Sermon on the Mount; Mark remembers the last charge given the disciples on Olivet, before the Master faded from their sight; John loves to linger over that meeting in the upper room, when the world-untroubled heart released all troubled ones from trouble. But all of the evangelists recall every detail of this exquisite incident that took place at the banquet in the house of that rich man of Bethany.

The host, one may justifiably conjecture, was the

leading merchant of his time. His caravans were ever on the road between Jerusalem and the cities of Egypt on the south, and the cities that clustered around Damascus upon the north. Simon dealt in wheat, and wool, and silk, in oil and wine, in spices from Arabia, and gold from Africa, and diamonds from India, and daily he increased in treasure. Tiring of the city, with its din and tumult, he built a rich man's house in the beautiful suburb of Bethany, and there he entertained his guests. From time to time every great city welcomes home the returning hero, the ruler or prince, who represents other lands. Little by little that first citizen of the Hebrew capital, Simon, came to be looked upon as the man who would do the honors for his fellow-men. In those days Jesus was the popular hero. Multitudes pressed and thronged to hear Him speak. The sheer beauty of His words cast a spell upon the multitude. He wove silken threads of truth and bound men as captives to His chariot. In Him the poor found a friend. To Him came the downtrodden, knowing that He would become a voice for their wrongs. The people gave Him their hearts, and thousands would have died for their Teacher. And when, at the end of an excited day, tired inside and tired out, Jesus withdrew to Bethany, this rich man, Simon, with his servants, came out to meet and greet the Master,

145

and took Him, as it were by force, and soon servants spread the feast.

When the news ran around that the great Teacher was at the rich man's house, merchants closed their shops, farmers left the plows in the field, women and children hurried to join the multitudes that filled Simon's house, and crowded his gardens, and overflowed into the street. Great is the power of the soldier! Wonderful the influence of the victor in battles upon land or sea! Most wonderful the power of the statesman, who receives triumphal processions, after some victory over oppression! But more wonderful still the majesty of goodness, the might of love, the regency of a radiant and luminous soul, like Jesus, who, all His life long went up and down the world doing good unto His fellows.

The beauty of this incident and its rich meanings can only be understood through contrasts. Our houses have doors against the chill and rigor of the winter. That house of Simon's was open and built for sunshine and the free movement of the currents of air. To our feasts come only invited guests; ancient feasts were public functions, and the proof that the host was poor was that he limited his invitations, and the proof that Simon was rich was that he had abundance and to spare for all who crossed the threshold of his house. In that far-off

146

era, also, tables were unknown. Guests reclined upon couches, and hours were spent in consuming an unending series of courses of rich foods. When the crowd was densest and there was scarcely room to move, and guests pushed and thronged one against another, a girl who was scarcely more than a child, a girl with a lovely, flower-face, but with robe of sackcloth, suddenly dropped upon her knees and put her arms above the feet of Jesus and bowed her head and burst into a flood of tears. A great silence fell upon the guests. Among those guests were men, perchance, who had reason to know that lovely girl. Perhaps one of them had broken down all the hedges that protect the sweet flowers of the heart in the garden of the soul.

Sometimes the garden gate is left open by the gardener in a thoughtless mood. Then enter the swine, and with tusk and snout root up the soil and grass and crush the snowdrop and the anemone and pull down the fragrant vines that creep over windows and walls. Soon the foul beasts finding the bubbling spring, wallow in the pure water and turn it into mire. They find a garden, they leave bleeding vines and bruised flowers. This girl had suffered much at the hands of evil men, who had placed in her hand the cup of flame, and with lying pledges lured her from the paths of peace into tropic jungles, where

147

blooms the scarlet upas flowers, flowers growing in fetid jungles, where death and putrefaction have their secret lair. But now at last all illusions have dissolved, the mirage has faded, the wreaths on the forehead of passion have withered, the lights have burned low in the socket, the night has fallen, the wind is chill, the storm clouds thicken, the windows begin to rattle, the wind sobs and sighs in the chimney. Voices of remorse threaten, and partly in a mood of fear and partly in shame, but most of all through sorrow and repentance, in a great, wild orgasm of confession, this sweet girl comes to herself! Her tears fall like rain upon the Master's feet.

Oh, these blessed tears! Not the dewdrop is so pure! This child feared lest her tears scald His person, and loosing her hair she made a veil behind which she could hide her face, and with the long tresses she wiped His feet, and took that sweet ointment, very precious, used only for great occasions, and broke the treasure-box for the Master. Sometimes men sweep a half-acre of red roses into one little vial, filled with their precious attar; and in those far-off days, experts distilled certain precious perfumes, and breaking not only the outer alabaster box, but that secret box of love, she poured out all the wealth of her soul upon the Master.

Be it remembered that in that era the debtor, in

The Bleeding Vine

asking mercy from his creditor, bowed at the feet
of his benefactor; that the slave and disciple knelt
at the foot of the master's couch and in embracing
the feet surrendered the very life in devotion to the
lord of the life. And in fulfilment of one of the
customs understood by all those guests, this woman
surrendered herself and by the symbolic act made
herself for evermore the slave to flawless purity and
perfect justice and the divine love of the Master.
It is only when we study the scenes and the unfold-
ing chapters in the life of this young girl that we
understand the exquisite beauty of an act that has
made immortal the doer. We know not her name,
we cannot measure the wealth of her love; the act
without represented the sentiment of the soul
within, but unconsciously she has built a monument
more enduring than marble or bronze. Her life
opened with a tender pastoral scene that we can re-
produce even as an expert can replace the amethyst
torn from its matrix and original setting. One night
her father returned from the city to his home in
the country. His daughter, wearing a simple white
dress, with one flower at her throat, met him at the
garden gate and clasped both hands about his arm.
She took him through the flower beds, not knowing
that she herself was the sweetest flower that had
bloomed under that sun. What anemones midst the

grass! What violets hidden under the leaves! There also were orange blossoms and on the same boughs the ripened fruit. And there with her own hands she had fastened the honeysuckle vine above the door and made the entrance to the house to be drenched with fragrance. She had spread the simple meal in a little summerhouse, and upon the white cloth she had placed the cold water from the spring. Then she lifted the leaves and showed him the strawberries she had just plucked and the thick cream all waiting, and the wheaten loaf, and trying to make him forget the toil of the day she drew him to his chair and put one arm around his shoulder and laid her face against his bronzed cheek and whispered, "Oh, father, I am so happy!" And crushing the sweet child to his breast the proud father forgot his tire and felt himself to be a king, and for one brief moment forgot his loneliness for her mother, so long since passed away. Wearing the child like a rose upon his heart, he bore himself like a king and walked the earth, a monarch among those who served.

Then came dark days. A serpent entered that garden. Mephistopheles conspired against young Marguerite. With fiendish skill he sought to break down the hedge and destroy the buttresses that protect virtue Then came a tragedy, oh, how black! It was the season for the games and sports and races of an age all too vulgar. All streets were thronged, and all race-tracks. The air was filled with the dust of chariots and runners and horsemen. Vendors of their wares lifted up shrill voices and cried aloud. And moving slowly through the scene went the Master and Lord of life. At last the Carpenter stayed His steps before a house of pleasure. Around one banqueting table sat a company of wild and reckless young men and women. And lo! The central figure, toward whose face all these half-drunken young men leaned, and to whom they stretched out the ripened grapes, the fresh figs, the fragrant sweetmeats, stands —that of the young girl of the garden, but with face, oh, how changed! And even as Jesus stays His steps beside that table she rises in her place, to drink a health, and drunken boys empty beakers into her overflowing glass, and the purple flood runs down and stains the cloth. Stopping before that table Jesus looked straight into the girl's eyes. Oh, those all-seeing eyes of Jesus! Eyes that knew all, understood all, and pitied all! No swords were in those eyes. No sparks of fire leaped forth. No arm was lifted to smite, but Jesus stood there, a great, dear presence, with rebuke of love and pain and disappointment! The girl stood transfixed, her lips parted, in wonder she stretched out that little, right hand, holding that enpurpled cup as if to ask, "Who art

151

thou?" Astounded, the revelers rise slowly to their feet. In astonishment they gaze first at the queen of the feast, and then at the strange Teacher, while they ask what these things may mean. Suddenly, she drops the goblet that, falling, breaks upon the table. She lifts her hands and tears away the scarlet flowers twisted in her hair. She strips the pearls from her throat and flings them upon the stones beneath. Still looking into the Master's eyes, she pulls off the rings and jeweled bracelets, and when the Master turns and covers His face with His hand because the pain of it was more than He could bear, she breathes forth one sobbing moan like a young and wounded thing, and sinks unconscious in the chair, as the shadows and dark night close around and veil the scene!

And now we behold another scene. Once more that young girl is back in her father's garden. The silent looks of that great Teacher had dissolved all the illusions of pleasure and sin. What had seemed ambrosia became the apples of Sodom, filled with ashes and soot. What once was the wine of Bacchus and the nectar of Venus, became as the droppings of asps and the poison of serpents. Those scarlet flowers that her lover had twisted into a wreath became like coals of fire, blistering her forehead. In her long pursuit of the god of pleasure, suddenly, that whom she had pursued turned, and instead of the face of some ideal youth she found she had embraced a toothless hag, and she shrieked aloud. In her black despair, she returned to the home, knowing she would find it empty because her sin had slain her father, and lo, the garden of her youth had come up to weeds, as toads and lizards ran across the garden walks. Fallen the vines from the bare windows! Gone all the sweet flowers! Rain had come through the roof. Mold was upon the walls. In an abandon of grief, she flung her face upon the garden grass and with dry sobs, her little fingers clutched the earth, while she called on death. Soon she plucked away each soft garment and in an old closet found sackcloth and black, and she hid herself until the night fell. Then, standing in the shadows, she stood in the outskirts of the multitude and listened to that strange Teacher, and once she drew nearer, and despite her veil found that the Master had recognized her. Suddenly He lifted His hand and, looking straight over the heads of other hearers to that place where she stood, He sent across the space one word for her heart alone: "I am come to seek and save that which is lost." Some inner voice whispered: "He speaks to you."

No mariner on a dark and stormy night upon a dangerous coast ever longed for the lighthouse that should lead into the harbor as that young girl had longed for the light, and now it had flamed forth. At last, the light had come! Shaken with joy, while hope and fear wrestled in her heart, she turned and fled back to that deserted garden, but all night long and all the next day the bells of hope kept ringing, and in her dreams she found herself again tossed in the dark upon the yeasty sea, and ever across the flood came that sweet and mellow bell, "I am come to seek and save that which is lost," and when she wakened it was as if a night of storm, with hissing winds and trembling earth, and sheeted flames and forked lightning had all passed, and left the flowers safe, and the garden sweet, and lo, the birds were singing again in the branches as a great peace stole into her heart.

When the night fell with transports of joy, she heard that the Master was at the house of the rich merchant, Simon, and entering with the great throng and concealing her face behind her robe, she suddenly finds herself beside His couch. Love always finds a way. The heart needs no guide and no protector. One look into His face told her heart that she had not deceived herself. What wonder words were those she heard? What did this mean that the Master should have asked Simon about the two creditors, and now, when the man who owed a vast debt, and the man whose debt was a trifle alike could pay nothing, that the creditor freely forgave them both? And what did this silence mean that fell upon the other guests at the question as to which debtor loved the benefactor most? And then came the answer, "I suppose that he loved most to whom most was forgiven." And in that moment she bowed her head and in a transport of joy she wept aloud as she heard the words, "Thy sins are forgiven thee. Go in peace." Wheresoever this story shall be told, it shall be a monument to her. Since that far-off time centuries have come and gone, but the story comes like a strain of sweet music sounding down the long aisles of time, and the fragrance of that box of ointment lingers and now perfumes all literature and lends sweetness to the wide-lying world.

The lessons of this exquisite scene in the life of the Redeemer are like flowers waiting to be plucked in God's rich garden. How plain it is that there are unrevealed treasures hidden under all the wreck of sin and shame. History tells us that the fire that followed the earthquake in Athens revealed, when the ashes were carried away, unsuspected veins of silver. But what hidden gold in every heart? In God's sight all men go forward, big with latent treasures. It is as if the farmer valued the field for its vegetables and grain, because his is a surface view. It is as if Simon had looked upon this sinning woman's life as upon a garden filled with weeds, thorns, and thistles, while the Lord of the garden, with all-seeing eye, pierced through the crust and saw beneath the soil with its mire-hidden veins of gold and crystals waiting to be cut into diamonds—as if all flashing rubies and sapphires were waiting to be uncovered.

Nor must we forget that other lesson, the judgment of perfect goodness upon the sins of the human heart, and the mercy of God's justice in whispering His verdict upon the deeds of the soul. Too often we have closed this revelation of the heart of God to open the Bible to statements about the wrath of an avenging law-giver. Philosophers have invoked the support of isolated texts, "Our God is a consuming fire," "The fear of the Lord is the beginning of wisdom," and so forth, forgetting that Jesus bore Himself in such a way as to reveal how God feels towards all erring ones who have left the paths of truth and virtue. As men go toward genius and greatness and the uttermost of holiness, they go toward gentleness in judgment. The Master and Lord of life, with His stainless perfection, was very pitiful. Sinful men would have fain stoned this girl. Perfect love, with instant pity, forgave her. Nor would He even permit her to tell her story. "Daughter"—ah, what a word was that! How long had she waited for some one to say the word that used often to fall from the lips of her revered father, long since dead. And now, that home word, "Daughter," that bosom pressure word, "My child," had fallen from the lips of the greatest among the holy, and the purest among the great. It was like water to a dying wanderer perishing of thirst in the desert. It was like music falling from the battlements of Heaven. What wonder words were these that fell upon her bleeding and broken heart: "Thy sins are forgiven thee, go in peace." In that moment the flare of lightning passed away, the black cloud on the horizon dissolved, the last echo of the midnight storm and tornado was hushed, the sun shone forth and in her vision she saw her father and mother coming across the grass in the souls' summerland, to take her into their arms and whisper welcome and lead her up unto the throne of mercy, not marble, the throne of love, and not law. And when the Master spoke the word "Forgiven" every wound was healed as she entered her Paradise, and her hot desert became an Eden garden.

THE FLAMING SWORD

Dr. Bushnell was born at Old Saybrook, Conn., in 1858; graduated from Yale University in the class of 1880; and after four years spent as Hooker fellow for special critical study, he entered the Congregational ministry in 1884. In 1888 he transferred to the Presbyterian fellowship, and, following a ministry at Rye, New York, was minister of Phillips and Madison Avenue Churches, New York City. Since 1900 he enjoyed a distinguished and fruitful ministry in the Westminster Presbyterian Church, Minneapolis. His volume of sermons, *Summit Views,* is aptly named and richly rewarding. A quiet ministry in a noisy age, busy about his work, but watchful of the trend of the times, he sees that the Garden of God is next door, but we are shut out by a stupidity which we think clever. As Arnold said of Goethe, he diagnoses the sick haste of the age, putting his finger on the secret and source of the wild restlessness which afflicts us like a fever. Physically it is the most comfortable age in history; spiritually one of the most uncomfortable—all because man thinks he knows more than God, and that he can make laws to suit himself. And the Flaming Sword flashes at the Garden Gate, as it will flash again at the Gate of Judgment!

THE FLAMING SWORD

JOHN EDWARD BUSHNELL, D.D.

WESTMINSTER PRESBYTERIAN CHURCH, MINNEAPOLIS

"So he drove out the man: and he placed at the east of the garden of Eden, cherubims, and a flaming sword which turned every way, to keep the way of the tree of life." Genesis 3: 24.

Viewed in the literal and material form these words baffle our imagination. Taken as a symbol of great historic facts they are almost overpowering in their conception. We do not know the way in which the first people of the race, in their simplicity, lived before they awakened to the ambitions and rivalries which came with advancing civilization. It was the childhood of the race in every sense of the word and, therefore, its state of mind was to that extent the happiness of immaturity. In the course of events life became more complex and troubled.

Whatever they enjoyed then and however much was lost through progress, we know that we are not in Eden at present. This is what concerns us, and also the question as to whether there is one which is awaiting us.

John Edward Bushnell, D.D.

I

What, then, is Eden to the modern mind, and where is it? If Jesus said: "The Kingdom of Heaven is within you," perhaps He also would have said the same of Eden. Surely there must be such a garden in our own hearts before any earthly garden, however beautiful, could give us full happiness. There always has been in the mind of man some faint vision at least of a more perfect life in this world.

It might seem almost as though we had by lineal descent inherited from our first parents some inborn idea of a life as sweet and happy as untroubled childhood, some garden in the East with fruits and flowers and friendly skies. Eden may be said to be in the blood of every man, we mean by that at least a dream of something better, a vision of a world that comes at last into its own, something unattained that has been lost out of our life which Providence designed for us.

In the darkest times peoples have hung their harps on the willows and wept, like the Jews of old separated from the homeland, but ever hoping and expecting that some day they would return. It takes the form of unrest, even under the best conditions. Things are never so good but that they ought to be better. It takes the form, among the young, of what

162

we express by that old word, the ideal. Man is ever seeking, but never finds the pot of gold at the end of the rainbow. "Man never is, but always to be blessed." His best work seems to him but a step toward the perfect.

Somewhere in the dim distance life on earth will be happier. There will be justice in place of wrong. Instead of murderous competition shall be coöperation. Instead of national animosities and hatreds shall be mutual respect and peace. Therefore the efforts made to bring it to peace, the lives sacrificed, the heroisms displayed, the prayers offered. Therefore the army of good men and women who have gone not with swords but with the Gospel to preach love and truth in God. So they cherish the angels' Christmas song of peace on earth, goodwill to men. It is deep down in the heart of the race.

At present the ideal seems further away than ever in some respects, and yet there are more people working, praying, and giving up their very lives to make it real again, to bring the world back to Eden, than ever before in the history of man. Somewhere, too, in the individual heart as well as in that of nations there is unrest, failure to find exactly that satisfaction in life which it gropes after. The East says: "It is not in me," and the West echoes back: "It is not in me."

John Edward Bushnell, D.D.

Eden, then, is a state of mind. It is like a fair, beautiful garden, for which the world is groping now, for which human souls are yearning, "a peace that passeth understanding," a life rich and full and free.

II

Eden lost. How? We may question the historical literalness of the ancient story of Genesis. None can dispute its Divine significance. Of each age it challenges interpretation.

We all have lost in our own lives our little garden. We lived in it for a while. We look back to it sometimes with longing. "Heaven lies about us in our infancy."

And as with persons so with peoples. Men, as they come to a fuller knowledge, their minds expanding and discovering, have lost simplicity out of life. They no longer are children, but straining, eager, pushing men, with more to tempt, more to appeal to the senses. The more there is to obtain, the greater grows the rivalry. When there was not much to buy there was not so much lust to get money. When there is much to be had when one can pay the price, the more fierce grows the struggle to possess the price.

Gandhi of India is trying to shut out the Western

The Flaming Sword

World and its civilization, its science and its inventions, and lead his people back to the primitive state as he sees how terrible this mechanical world of ours has become in its thirstings and fightings, its tramplings upon the weaker in order that the strong may climb. Men have sacrificed the real for the unreal, the substance for the shadow. They have thought that Eden lay yonder. God placed it elsewhere.

As education has advanced, as men have eaten of the tree of knowledge of good and evil, they have enlarged their life and brought into subjection many of the material forces. Yet with all the benefits and possibilities has come much that has drawn men away from the Eden of their dreams. Pride has come in, with doubts and unbelief in the things unseen and eternal. In these days, instead of leading us on into the infinite and up to God, civilization is very largely drawing in its lines and actually limiting men's visions and confining their thoughts to the material. Eden is not there.

So men, finding themselves in this world, enriched in knowledge, adorned by the products of its sciences, comfortable and beautiful in its homes and their furnishings, still have the haunting dream. Something has been unachieved which the race innately has felt to be in the great designs of creation.

In the allurements of life, in the haste to possess

and the greed to enjoy, in "the lust of the flesh, and the lust of the eyes, and the pride of life," life becomes fearfully, painfully sordid and selfish. The very things that should be blessings become foes. The things that ought to make people grateful make them unthankful. The more the world brings to us the more difficult to restrain the human heart from vanity and pride and desire for more. Thence come wars.

There never has been a time, since Cain killed his brother, that the human race has stopped fighting. And as one authority said: "The nineteenth century in that respect was the worst of all." We can see that this is so for, with its great equipments, its organized forces and the lust for empire, the greed and pride of life, that one great century was red and the fury ceased not until it took possession of the twentieth century and wrought the greatest havoc and reached its very climax of woe, so awful that the only redeeming hope that is left out of it all is that the very horror of it may mean the death of all its brood.

But do we not have in our world to-day the conflict of those other passions which are as destructive in their way as those displayed upon the battlefield? Their consequences are in some respects more pitiable. That is the world we live in, and Eden never seemed farther away from men's vision and faith than in this most enlightened, most scientific, most learned, and richest age in all human history. And what has brought it to pass but man seeking his own and caring not for his brother and unheeding the Christ of Calvary.

But yet there is an Eden. Somehow, in all the dance of circumstances, in all the rage for pleasure, in all the sway of the things that are sensual and voluptuous, in the midst of the mad rush for wealth and excitement and greed for pleasure, in the decline even of religion itself, there still remains in the human heart a belief that this world is not to be given over to the things that destroy, that heroism is not a thing of the past, that there must arise a conquering desire for a world of more kindly sentiments, where men and women who speak different tongues may be able to live together and learn to enjoy one another, that righteousness will come to its own, that those who stand for the right and dare to speak the truth will be heard. The pledge is in the sacrifice of Love Divine upon the cross.

III

What, then, is the flaming sword? As it turns in the hand of the angel it tells us that the garden has not been destroyed, that it is still there while man wanders afield and seeks outside its gates the object of his desires. This very thing that excludes men also shows them the way home. If we have lost anything of value we are self-banished. We did not have to go, but we defied the everlasting laws that lie at the heart of things.

Men are not happy because they have violated the principles on which happiness depends. It takes the world a long time to learn that it cannot construct rules of its own to take the place of those that flash from that burning steel. There are certain things that are right and right obeyed is the secret of wisdom. Man cannot change the order, annul the decrees that are eternal, and make unrighteousness profitable. He cannot make the wages of sin into currency to buy happiness.

We may make as many statutes as we please, decreeing the rules that shall bring health to the body, that henceforth carbolic acid shall be an innocent beverage for the thirsty to drink, that God's commands are abrogated, that the lie shall be as productive of good as the truth, that virtue and integrity are not to be regarded as essential to national welfare, that we may say both "Good Lord" and "Good Devil." Referendum may be made to the people to suspend the Ten Commandments or

The Flaming Sword

the precepts of the Sermon on the Mount. But the flashing sword is at the gate. You cannot enter in defiance of those things that never change, for God is God and truth is truth, sin is sin and hatred is not the same as love.

The wise physician is sitting down with a youth to tell him how to possess the strongest body and fit himself physically for the labors that are before him. He holds up to him sensibly certain general principles which govern health and the preservation of life. He says to him in effect: "This is the gate of your Eden, a rounded, perfect manhood. Obey these laws and you enter. Defy them and you stay without."

The father is bidding farewell to his boy who is going into the great world out of his sight. He has learned some things by experience as well as from the books. He has his ideals for his son. He covets for him a splendid success, nobly won, with the esteem and affection of his fellow men. He exalts before his vision the things of value, the things that make for character, for which he must make sacrifices at times in order to obtain them. Through that gate is the Eden of a happy, satisfied life, blessed and a blessing to the world.

The business house has its rules for successful industry. Law guards the gate also of the Eden of the commercial world, that of industry, obligation, patience, and self-restraint which sacrifices the things that injure one's capacity for work, that becloud one's mind for thinking, that make one less capable mentally of his best.

There is a flaming sword in whatever direction you look for Eden. It is for us to interpret the shining symbol.

IV

The sheathing Day! How long will the world stay outside the beautiful garden of its quest, content to be restless, warring, hating, sinning, substituting the laws of men for those of God, thinking that it can purchase peace?

Let us make no mistake about it. Happiness is found only when the eternal truths are held in reverence and the everlasting laws obeyed. We may think that we can suspend the rule that what one sows that shall he reap. But the sword is at the gate. The farmer must obey the laws that govern the land or accept an empty granary.

We cannot but feel to-day that all we have, all we have learned, all that our labors have brought to us, have failed to bring us that which we in our heart of hearts know to be what we have a right to seek for and demand. Life should be happier, more comfortable. Toil should be made to become pleasanter as well as more profitable. Men should live together in human society without this constant irritation and anger. The forces of evil should not have such sway and brazenly defy virtue and honor.

Is it not written: "For the earnest expectation of the creation waiteth for the revealing of the sons of God"? That day lies beyond the unrest, the loss of faith, the widespread despair, the prevalence of evil that destroys, that robs youth of virtue and life of strength. To bring that day Christ gave His life.

Not until the heart is humbled and is willing to bow to the great truths which, because they have been long defied, have long afflicted them by their penalties, can men reach the haven of their hopes. When earth's people shall recognize the law of righteousness and of love, then shall the tumult cease as well as the jarrings and the crimes and the things that shame. There is a gate by which every nation, every town, every soul must pass if it would find that self-fulfilment which it has the right and duty to claim, that sublime consummation which is written in the beneficent plan and glows in the bountiful promises of our Father God.

John Edward Bushnell, D.D.

Yet there may be no sheathing Day for Eden's sword. Rather by faith we may see it now delivered into the wounded hand of One returning from great wars, victorious. No longer does it tell of exile from true life, but it beckons homeward where through the gate Christ marshals back His own.

ON LOVING AN ENEMY

A native of Nova Scotia—born at New Ross in 1874—trained at University of King's College, Windsor, with postgraduate work in philosophy at Columbia University, Dr. Norwood was ordained to the priesthood of the Episcopal Church in 1898. His first work was that of a missionary at Neil's Harbor, Cape Breton: then a curate of St. Luke's Church, Hubbards; an assistant rector of Trinity Church, Montreal; rector of Memorial Church, London, Ontario; whence he came to St. Paul's Church, Overbrook, Philadelphia, where his ministry has grown and gathered power since 1917. Dr. Norwood is a preacher of the order of poets, not a poet-preacher who weaves wreaths of flowery emptiness, but a seer to whom the multi-colored world is a Divine parable, aglow with light and loveliness and moving to moral and spiritual ends. His angle of insight, his method of approach to truth, his fresh, joyous, quick-darting fancy, betray the poet-soul revealing itself now in sermons that search like a white flame, now in books of poems like *His Lady of the Sonnets* and *The Piper and the Reed,* now in a drama like *The Witch of Endor.* The present sermon is preaching of a very real kind, and only a poet could thus link the back of God seen by Moses in dim vision with the bent back of the happy Burden-Bearer, in whom God became man that man may become godlike. One feels in the sermon a glow of that incommunicable grace which invests the man and his preaching with the lure of a unique and compelling charm.

ON LOVING AN ENEMY

ROBERT NORWOOD, D.D.

ST. PAUL'S EPISCOPAL CHURCH, OVERBROOK, PHILADELPHIA

"And I shall take away mine hand, and thou shalt see my back parts: but my face shall not be seen." Exodus 33: 23.

"But I say unto you, Love your enemies, bless them that curse you, and pray for them that despitefully use you, and persecute you." Matt. 5: 44.

In the portions of scripture read this morning the picture of God is given. It is the same picture. It is the picture of the goodness of God in human action. How would God act if He came down to earth as a man? Would He talk about His omnipotence? Would He force people to be conscious that He was the mighty God of the universe?

"Yes, that is what He would do," say a great number of people. "We would know He was God if He came down with His omnipotence; but if He did not, how would we recognize Him? He would have to show us His face—the face of a king, not the back of a servant. We should expect Him to walk on water; if he did not, we would not believe He was God. We should expect Him to turn water into wine; if He did not, we would not believe He was

175

God. We should expect Him to use thunder and lightning on His enemies, calling down from the heaven, which He had left for our sakes, the fires of His wrath and terrible judgments."

How would God act if He came down to earth? There are people who say that He would act in a very beautiful and simple way. He would cause His goodness to pass before our faces. He would not frighten us with His splendor, but woo us with His gentle love and tenderness. He would come, not as a king, but as a servant. He would not show the face of a king. He would show a back for bearing burdens. He would not bother at all about advertising Himself with signs and wonders. He would rely only on His goodness, because the goodness of God is the allness of God. If you could take away the goodness of God from His omnipotence, the result would be the devil. It is goodness with omnipotence that makes omnipotence divine. He would cause His goodness to pass before us.

We have been listening to the words of a man whom the ages have regarded, and still regard, as the goodness of God, believing that God at last, in the fullness of time, came to earth in the person of Jesus. Of Him many stories have been written, many things said—things that are not always consistent and, therefore, cannot be held as equally true. Some of these stories indicate average notions of greatness which are fundamentally wrong because so many people hold that power is greatness. To such the thought of goodness as greatness is absurd. People like these are seekers of the sign—so described by the Master when he called them "an adulterous generation." It is possible that, at bottom, the fall of Judas was due to this vulgarity of insisting on omnipotence.

This attitude of mind towards omnipotence is revealed in the schoolboy's muscular demonstrations—the cutting of a cart-wheel before his sweetheart. We accept this thing in a schoolboy because he has not yet come to the age of putting away childish things, but it is amazing that, at this hour, so many sons of God express this mind in their interpretation of the New Testament. They must have every miracle literally true because, if you take away the miracles—the signs of power—you strike at the goodness of Christ; as though goodness were revealed in power.

Not in this spirit was the Master described by Matthew, quoting Isaiah: "Behold my servant, whom I have chosen; my beloved, in whom my soul is well pleased: I will put my Spirit upon him, and he shall shew judgment to the Gentiles. He shall not strive, nor cry; neither shall any man hear his voice in the streets. A bruised reed shall he not break, and smoking flax shall he not quench, till he send forth judgment unto victory."

As for the Master's opinion of those who stress omnipotence as the evidence for God, the Gospels abound with his words of rebuke. He has described these seekers in his "Verily I say unto you, They have their reward." They get what they are after. They get notice. They want to attract attention to themselves because they are selfish and vain and small, and they assume that God, also, wants to attract attention to Himself by stunts, stressing omnipotence instead of love.

It is fair to consider that the task of a disciple is not easy. It was not easy for Moses, who evidently thought more of rocking mountains and flaming skies than he did of God's goodness. It took him a long while to learn to be content with the vision of God's back, to get along without the vision of God's face. One day he came to see that only as a man is identified with God's back can he see God's face. The way to the knowledge of God's power is along the path of God's goodness.

That is how the Master prepared his disciples for their ministry, and it is still his method of preparing his friends for their work in this world, for the words that he spoke to his first group of disciples apply to every group. A disciple is a man chosen by God to represent God. That is all there is to Christianity. Of course there are the subsidiary things—things to be added when the essential lesson has been learned. When the goodness of God has been learned, the power of God will come as a matter of course; but seek first His goodness.

It came upon me like a beam of sunlight in a dark room, as we said the General Confession, that the knowledge of the goodness of God is exactly what the Church has wanted us to get when we are asked to say, "We bless thee for our creation, preservation, and all the blessings of this life." We do bless God for creation, because Christ teaches us that God has created us to manifest Him, that we may be the vehicles of His splendor, partners with Him in the manifestation of what He wants to give everybody. "We thank Thee for the wonderful destiny Thou hast chosen for us. We thank Thee that Thou hast called us to be Thy ministers and stewards. Wherever we are, this is our highest rôle. Thou hast chosen us to be Thy voice, Thy hands, Thy feet. Thou hast chosen us to be Thy back. But, above all, we thank Thee for Thine inestimable love in the redemption of the world by our Lord Jesus Christ. And, we beseech Thee, give us that due sense of all thy mercies, that our hearts may be unfeignedly thankful; and that we show forth thy praise, not only with our lips, but in our lives."

Christianity is not a creed, but a life. The creed is a beautiful thing—a decoration, if you will. It is a jewel in our life, but life is the crown. Christianity is a life. It is based on the belief that God can become man. A disciple of Jesus Christ is a man inspired by the example of his master—a man who carries on and says, "God has become man in me. God is using me as a veil in order that, as it is parted by my life here on this planet, people may see His goodness."

Oh, if we in our squabbles could only see that! If we could only see that the right thing is for everybody to be loyal to the life and let the rest go.

What is divinity but Jesus? What is divinity but the goodness of God? Do you know of any other kind of divinity? Did I not say, if you separate goodness from omnipotence, you have the devil? The essence of your divinity and mine is that same kind of goodness, and the Master is our authority. Be perfect. You won't be in a minute. There will be barriers ahead of you, disciplines and tests and challenges. Go on. There are things you can do. Begin to practise. Love your enemy. The goodness of God will go out into the world through your name if you become one who never answers back, never gossips, is never vindictive. Arise and try it. The goodness of God will pass by in your manhood, if, instead of being critical of your neighbor, you become the gentle man, the burden-bearer.

There are many things for us to acquire on this planet. Some may acquire faith, some wealth, some a life of ease and redemption from toil; but there is only one thing for a Christian to acquire—a fact that is summed up in a little verse I found years ago in an old album of a country home in Nova Scotia. I think it ran like this:

> When you were born a helpless child,
> You only cried while others smiled.
> So live that when you come to die,
> You then may smile while others cry.

To be remembered as a tender presence, as always devoted, always understanding, always kind; to be remembered as the healer, the helper, the one who was hospitable, the one whose hand was always on the gate of opportunity for friendship: surely that is the highest reward. This is in store for those who have listened to the Master in the Sermon on the Mount: "It was said to you of old time, Love your friends and hate your enemies; but I say unto you, if you would let the goodness of God through into the world by your body, which is the means of your grace, then learn to be the lover, the forgiver, the compassionate one. As your Father in heaven is revealed in me, so let your Father in heaven be revealed in you."

"But," you say, "it cannot be done."

I answer, "It was done once."

"Ah," you say, "that was different."

I answer, "Wherein is the difference? Certainly not in the mind of him who said, 'Follow me' . . . 'All power is given unto me' . . . 'As my Father hath sent me, even so send I you.'" It was done once, and it can be done again. You can do it. How? Begin at the narrow gate. What is that? I think it is in loving our enemies. That is about the hardest thing one can do who would cause the goodness of God, through himself, to pass before a world. Face that fact. It is hard—hard to the point of Gethsemane and crucifixion, so hard that failures are inevitable among those who begin. Such a beginning is true conversion, for "every one that loveth is born of God." To look at the goodness of God; to be content with it and let His omnipotence go—His baffling, mysterious omnipotence; to be content with the life of love and service and the vision of the back instead of the vision of the face; to cease to be a wrangler, a backbiter, an arguer about the nature of God—whether He does this or whether He does that; and to love without limit as the Master loved: surely this is conversion. This is the beginning of the path through the little gate that leads unto life.

Do you recall, my comrades, the tender thought that Browning places in the heart of Karshish, who is concluding his letter that tells of how he met Lazarus and, through that, was led to see the goodness of God in the Galilean? Browning must have been thinking just as we have been thinking together this morning; but surely his mind is as our mind when he distinguishes between power and love and puts the emphasis where it belongs and where the Master places it—where we must place it—where Moses placed it when God caused all His goodness to pass before him and left His omnipotence out:

> The very God! think, Abib; dost thou think?
> So, the All-Great, were the All-Loving too—
> So, through the thunder comes a human voice
> Saying, "O heart I made, a heart beats here!
> Face, my hands fashioned, see it in myself!
> Thou hast no power nor may'st conceive of mine,
> But love I gave thee, with myself to love,
> And thou must love me who have died for thee!"

And now we are come to this moment of consecration, to the life of the goodness of God. Let us bow our heads and say, "Teach us to live as Thou didst live, O generous Love that was made man, manifesting Thy goodness in a cross and its redeeming power. Speak to us as, on a day of old, Thou didst speak to Thy first disciples, and give us again to understand Thy words: 'Ye have heard that it hath been said, Thou shalt love thy neighbor and hate thy enemy; but I say unto you, Love your enemies . . . that ye may be the children of your Father, that you may be God in human form, as I, your Master, am God in human form.' "

Let us pray:

In humility and yet in eagerness for all tests we come to Thee, O Master of men, who didst make the goodness of our Father pass by in the form of the back that bore a cross. We come to Thee because Thou didst live the life, because we want to live it, knowing that Thy grace is sufficient for us and Thy strength is made perfect in our groping, stumbling efforts. We ask for just this one thing this morning—that we may learn how to be kind. It is easy to be kind to those who are kind to us. That is nothing. Even the Pharisees are kind like that. But it is only Thy power and grace revealed in mankind, when some one is kind to those who are unkind to him. It seems hard, Master, but Thou didst do it. It is not enough to say "Master, master." We must be the Master, and be disgusted

On Loving an Enemy

with ourselves if we are not. We are such hypocrites. We are so ostentatious and so proud, Master. Place Thy hand upon our heads—our poor, bowed, humble heads, and forgive us our hypocrisy. Send us forth for one week of lovingkindness. Amen.

THE RADICALISM OF JESUS

Dr. McKeehan is one of the outstanding younger men of the American pulpit—the youngest included in this volume—who is rapidly making his way into the front rank. Born on a farm near Newport, Pa., in 1897, after attending schools and academies in his county, he studied with a relative of his family, Prof. J. P. Mahaffy, Provost of the University of Dublin. Subsequently he studied at Valparaiso University, and after graduating from the Theological Seminary of the Reformed Church, he became pastor of St. Paul's Reformed Church, Dallastown, Pa. Last year he preached in a number of English pulpits and at Oxford University, on his way as delegate of the Reformed Church to the World Council of Churches at Zurich. He is editor of a volume of *Great Modern Sermons*, and author of *The Patrimony of Life*—sermons reminiscent of the Gunsaulus-Hillis type of preaching, but with an accent and emphasis uniquely his own. A young man in the morning of his career, he is a spokesman of one of the first Christian communions in America to emphasize a Christocentric faith, at once a focus of fellowship and a prophecy of unity.

THE RADICALISM OF JESUS

HOBART D. McKEEHAN, S.T.M.

ST. PAUL'S REFORMED CHURCH, DALLASTOWN, PA.

"Ye have heard it said of old time, but I say unto you."
Matt. 5: 21, 22.
"From within, out of the hearts of men, evil thoughts proceed." Mark 7: 21.

Jesus of Nazareth was the greatest of all Radicals, and His spirit is the most radical force in human history. By both precept and example he went to the very root of the moral and spiritual life. Pressing beneath the apparent, he unveiled the actual. Passing beyond the symptoms of either health or disease, righteousness or sin, He revealed the primal causes. His claim as Teacher and Leader in individual and social life was asserted upon the ruling motives which actuate the hearts of men and women. Like all true radicals Jesus went to the source and origin of every problem. And like all true radicals He had no fear of the triumph and implications of ultimate Truth. The more one studies the life and teachings of Jesus with a serious and unprejudiced mind the greater grows his conviction of the unparalleled radicalism of the Master.

And yet the radicalism of Jesus is profoundly unique. In searching out the hidden springs of thought and conduct, in probing after all primal causes either of light or of darkness, *Jesus is always dealing with persons*. Other teachers have declared that the weal and woe, the joy and pain of individual and communal life is bound up with educational, political, or economic régimes. But Jesus declared that they were determined not by circumstances, but by men. And this uniqueness of Christ stands in bold relief when one considers Him in comparison with any other teacher.

"We study Aristotle," says Carnegie Simpson, "and are intellectually edified thereby; we study Jesus and are, in the profoundest way, spiritually disturbed. When we had thought intellectually to examine Him, we find He is spiritually examining us." This is the uniqueness of His radical disposition and proposals. A man may indeed study Jesus with intellectual impartiality—but no man can study Jesus seriously and do so with moral neutrality! He must agree or disagree with His proposals. He must accept or reject His spirit. Ultimately there is no neutral ground.

Perhaps one can find the radicalism of Jesus set

forth in no more striking fashion than by comparing His teaching with that of His Hebrew predecessors and contemporaries. Reverencing the past, loving the Law, ever listening to the wise ancestral voices of prophets, priests, poets, and kings, Jesus was by no means disrespectful toward either the Church or the State. In the truest possible sense He came to fulfil rather than to destroy. Nevertheless, He poured new meaning into old thought-forms, new wine into old wine skins. And because He studied the roots rather than the branches, because He dealt with motives rather than with actions, with causes rather than with effects, and insisted upon a transformed rather than a conformed life,—because of this, I say, the proposals of Jesus constitute the most radical body of teaching in the history of the world. I am not thinking, however, of the doctrines and dogmas which have long been promulgated as the major portion of the teaching of the Church. I am not suggesting that there is anything unusually radical in much that has been taught concerning Jesus. But who will question the radicalism of Jesus Himself—of His teaching and example among men! Never man so spake—never did man so live! And because no man has ever spoken like Jesus and none have lived like Him, it is perhaps not inexplicable why so few have ever understood Him! His own age did not understand Him. His own family did not understand Him! He was difficult to understand because His attitude toward life was so radical, His attitude toward personalities so innovating, His attitude toward tradition and orthodoxy so skeptical, His cardinal propositions of doctrine so revolutionary, and yet His communion with His Father so unclouded and unbroken as to make Him forever solitary and unique in all spiritual matters. Is it any wonder that Nazareth did not understand Jesus? Or that the representatives of organized business, organized religion, and organized politics united to crucify Him at Jerusalem when He was at least partially understood! And is it not plain that the major portion of the church does not seem to understand Him, even to-day?

Consider but a few fragments of what was and is involved in the attitude and teaching of Jesus. *His attitude toward life itself was radical!* He was an optimist. He was a Man of joy. The New Testament itself is the most joyous and optimistic book in the world. It begins with a glowing star and the song of Angels. It ends with a shout of triumph! Doubtless much which controversialists have read into the New Testament and much which the dogmatists have woven around the New Testament is *not* joyous and optimistic. But I am not concerned with these things. I am thinking of the Evangel itself. And I am certain that Jesus, as the author of the Evangel, was a lover of life. He drew no sharp distinction between earth and heaven. He believed in life—full, free, creative, and abundant life! And the New Testament is not the biography of a recluse, but of a virile Man among men. As Principal Jacks rightly says: "Christianity fails through the loss of its radiant energy. There is that in the Gospel which is akin to the song of the skylark and the babbling of brooks!"

Consider also how radical was Jesus' *attitude toward persons*. He looked upon men and women as an end in themselves and not as means to an end. He saw in all ranks and conditions of society the promise of a divine brotherhood and sonship. Emerson has said that Christ alone in history rightly estimated the greatness of man. Man's success or failure, said Jesus, is not determined by the place and conditions into which he happens to be born, but by the choices which he must constantly make.

Aideen, in that strange and fascinating novel, *The Unpardonable Sin*, presents Jesus' point of view, saying: "What you have been, you have been. What you have done, you have done. But what you are is what you choose to be. No spirit can take away your power over yourself. The present is greater than the past and the future greater than the present."

Against the arbitrary castes of sex or station in society and the cynicism either of wealth or of learning, Jesus arose in deep revolt. The Greeks were typical of the Ancient world when they spoke of women as being the result of nature's failure to make men, and of artisans and mechanics as being incapable of any virtue. And into such a world of thought and outlook came Jesus, announcing not only that persons are of equal worth before God, but that personality is the crowning triumph of God's creative endeavors. To men and women of all stations of life and all grades of culture He brought a revelation of their divine origin, their infinite worth, their unbounded possibilities and their endless and unaging existence.

The *skepticism* of Jesus reveals His radical nature. That is not to say that the Master was a rationalist, that He was not a man of reverence and faith. He was, on the contrary, the most perfect example of faith, of absolute trust in God, in all history. No man ever believed in the goodness of God and in the essential friendliness of the universe as Jesus believed. Nevertheless, though He was not a rationalist, He certainly was not a sentimentalist. He was never the victim of a venerated but irrational tradition.

194

The Radicalism of Jesus

He was thoughtful, reflective, searching and challenging. Read anew the initial discourses of His public ministry and notice with what frequency they were punctuated with the word, "Why?" Indeed, I am led to feel that Frederick W. Norwood does not overstate the case when he says that "almost half of the discourses of Jesus, as they have come down to us, are challenges of the orthodoxy of His own day!"

The cardinal doctrine and proposal of Jesus portrays a most radical innovation. I mean, of course, His doctrine and proposal of the Kingdom of Heaven. Almost wholly absent in all of the historic creeds, always a minor consideration in the realm of dogma, and occupying, even to-day, a very subordinate place in popular preaching, yet the doctrine and proposal of the Kingdom of Heaven constitute the major portion of Christ's Evangel to men and nations. And it may be that secular thinkers and historians have noted this fact with greater insight than Churchmen have.

"The doctrine of the Kingdom of Heaven," says Herbert George Wells, "which was the main teaching of Jesus, and which plays so small a part in the Christian creeds, is certainly one of the most revolutionary doctrines that ever stirred and changed human thought. It is small wonder if the world at that time failed to grasp its full significance and recoiled in dismay from even a half apprehension of his tremendous challenges to the established habits and institutions of mankind." But what we must see is that Jesus believed in the Kingdom which He proclaimed, that He was its perfect incarnation and that He trusted nothing save spiritual forces for its complete realization.

And because He proposed so radical a doctrine as that of the Kingdom of Heaven and placed such implicit faith in spiritual forces—truth, justice, and love—for its realization, Jesus went to the Cross! Rejected by those to whom His doctrine was proclaimed, by organized religion no less than by organized business and organized politics, He wrote His doctrine in unfading letters of crimson. "But," says Giovanni Papini, "only with the blood in our veins can truth be written permanently on the pages of earth so that it will not fade under men's footsteps or under the rainfall of centuries. The Cross is the rigorously necessary consequence of the Sermon on the Mount. Everything must be paid for, the good at a higher price than evil; and the greatest good, which is love, must be paid for by the greatest evil in men's power." And it was the very learned Dean of St. Paul's who, in his recent Ascension Day Sermon, reminded his hearers that "Christ could not have gone on living on earth because there never have been wanting evil men who would have crucified Him afresh, or otherwise slain Him, pretending that they were doing God a service. Such is the way in which our misguided race has always treated its greatest benefactors, those of whom the world was not worthy."

And we modern Christians must remember this fact: that the religion of Jesus is a religion for heroes, and that for us, as for our Master, the only road leading to spiritual triumph is the Via Dolorosa. The man who accepts and proclaims the doctrine of the Kingdom of Heaven with understanding and seriousness, who trusts in the ultimate triumph of spiritual forces, and who, therefore, lives and thinks above the average and ahead of his time— that man must pay the price!

And yet is it not amazing that so many men have been willing to pay the price and face a cross? And is it not the most hopeful sign of the twentieth century that Christ is persuading men, as never before, of the essential truth of His proposals, and that the volunteers to His Army of Love were never so numerous and never more serious? Behold! nowhere, save in Christ's doctrine of the Kingdom, have men been able to find a real basis for a Parliament of Man and a Federation of the World.

Even so pessimistic a thinker as Bertrand Russell,

whom no one would venture to call a friend of the Church, when he comes to consider the proposals of Jesus is wont to admit that "if all men could summon up the courage and the vision to live in this way in spite of obstacles and discouragement, there would be no need for the regeneration of the world to begin by political and economic reform; all that is needed in the way of reform would come automatically, without resistance, owing to the regeneration of individuals." And such a confession coming, as it does, from one who is considered hostile to the Church, is certainly significant.

Nevertheless, there remains a final aspect of the proposals of Jesus which makes Him more radical still. *He alone of all earth's teachers provides the resources that make possible the attainment of His ideals and standards.* Moses offers Law; Plato teaches Truth—but Jesus brings God to men and men to God! Jesus gives men no Hill of Difficulty to climb without first giving them the needed strength wherewith to climb it. He calls men to no moral battle without first supplying the weapons which make them invincible. He asks them to walk no hazardous pathway over which He himself has not gone before them. In Jesus and in His Evangel the unseen becomes the real, and God becomes man's Ally and Contemporary!

The Radicalism of Jesus

This, then, constitutes at least an outline picture of the radical Vision and Evangel of the Man of Galilee—the most elemental, most searching, and most challenging Soul who ever trod the human ways of earth! And, to-day, as more than nineteen centuries ago, He calls to a distracted world and to a church which has ever been known by His name, but not always by His Spirit, saying: "Why call ye me, Lord, Lord, and do not the things that I say?"

O Church of the living God, we are summoned to give answer; are we Christian enough to take Jesus and His proposals in earnest? Are we noble enough and heroic enough to put first things first and to seek that Kingdom which Jesus proclaimed and then died to reveal? Is God, the Father of Jesus and through Jesus our Father, so real in our experience and so controlling in our convictions as to permit us to trust absolutely in spiritual forces for the attainment of a Kingdom of holy love? If so, then we are the worthy heirs of Christ's radical Spirit and the torchbearers in His Triumphal procession up the Hills of Light. If not, then we *may* be *religious,* but we are *not Christian!*

THE YOUNGER GENERATION

While we are listening to the man in the pulpit—"the Speaking Man," as Carlyle would say—it is not inappropriate to hear a sermon from the pew, especially when a great and wise teacher talks to us both plainly and hopefully about our young people, whose ways of thinking and doing often fill us with dismay. Dr. Hawkes came to the chair of mathematics in Columbia from Yale University in 1910, and was made Dean of the College eight years later, having won distinction as a teacher and as the author of standard text-books in algebra and geometry. His favorite field of research had been hypercomplex numbers, but since his elevation to the deanship he has become deeply interested in the hypercomplex state of mind in which young men find themselves when torn between the old pieties of the home and the shifting moral standards and changing vision in religious ideals in the modern world. He believes it is possible to live spiritually and think scientifically, uniting the old values of the spirit with the new vision of the world and its laws; and to that end he is a wise mentor of bewildered youth. Out of his experience as teacher, friend and confidant of young men he speaks in this sermon, and when laymen preach such sermons it is time for preachers to look well to their laurels.

THE YOUNGER GENERATION

HERBERT E. HAWKES

DEAN OF COLUMBIA COLLEGE, NEW YORK

Matt. 16: 25.

My remarks this evening are not from the point
of view of a student of current theological or religious
questions. I am quite untouched by the turmoil of
the ecclesiastical world as to whether a certain clause
of the creed shall be interpreted in this way or in
that way. To me the creeds are the great anthems
of religion which had their origin in the attempt of
men to express in language the aspirations of their
hearts for a closer walk with God. I will sing the
anthem and feel the same aspiration that they felt
without raising any question of the exact and literal
meaning of the words. As well refuse to sing a beautiful song of love or beauty until one can literally
accept the scientific accuracy of its words as to refuse
to join in these great symphonies of religious expression. But this is merely an observation by a layman who has already said that he is not versed in
theology.

Herbert E. Hawkes

My theme may be expressed in the following words: *"For whosoever will save his life shall lose it, and whosoever will lose his life for my sake shall find it."*

It is my privilege to meet on very intimate terms hundreds of young people and to discuss with them every imaginable question that arises in the experience of young men between the ages of 15 and 25. I wish to talk to you for a few minutes about the younger generation. It is easy to be dogmatic when speaking on this subject. It is easy for us to criticize our fathers as being narrow, somewhat intolerant, and insistent on what seems to us an outworn philosophy of living. It is even easier to observe in our children those tendencies which seem to indicate only frivolity and abandon. Just now, however, I do not wish to debate or to criticize, but to analyze. What are the outstanding facts in our society that will help *us* to understand the younger generation, and will help *them* to understand themselves? And what is the underlying reason for these facts?

During recent years men in every field of thought and activity have shown a strong tendency to get away from the principles and canons that have been generally assumed and accepted for generations.

The painter nowadays is likely to attempt to express his mood by a use of color and by a method

204

of composition that seems to many a conservative observer grotesque, meaningless, and untrue. Much of our modern music does not pretend to get anywhere. One sound follows another and the entire succession is intended only to express in a charming manner the phantasy or emotion of the composer. But so far as musical form and order or development is concerned, there is no such thing in the music that we usually call modern. The composer is concerned with expressing himself rather than with developing a musical subject.

Up to date education places great emphasis on cultivating the individuality of the child instead of acquainting him with the rudiments of method and information that have in the past nourished and equipped the race for their life work. On coming to school in the morning the modern child is requested to tell the teacher what he would like to study (if anything) that day. Each topic is preferably taken up from the point of view of its functioning in the immediate experience of the child. The functioning of the subject in the experience of the human race is secondary. The orderly exposition of a subject of study is not the method of the present-day teacher. The present interest of the pupil is the guiding principle, and it is hoped that if the child remains in school long enough his individual interest will go the

rounds of reading, arithmetic, and so on, and finally
equip him with the knowledge that he needs for his
career. But thorough and consecutive progress in a
subject of study is not the method.

The test of the true and the good in the philosophy
of to-day is found in its practicability. An act is right
if it results in satisfaction to those concerned, not
if it conforms to some recognized standard of right.
Anything that works in practice is thereby justified.

Our poetry is as formless as our music and our
novels are cross sections of the lives of the characters,
without the sense of solidity and universality that
characterized our best novels of years past. Nothing
is too sordid or too mean to be expressed in full detail without leaving anything to the reader's imagination. Everything is told.

Our manners, too, are without the reserve that has
often been supposed to be the mark of good breeding.
There is little that cannot be said and done without
compunction or shame. Principles either do not exist
or are not considered of weight. The modern individual follows the impulse to behave in the manner
that seems most convenient at the time. For him,
law is something to be obeyed only if it comes handy.

This is the kind of world and atmosphere to which
our younger generation is introduced and in which
they are working out their salvation. In art, music,

and poetry, in education and philosophy the idea of
conformity to a standard outside of the individual is
not thought of. In fact the existence of any such
standard is frequently denied. Religion, dress,
amusement, all reveal a similar falling away from a
regard for any fundamental principle, and a corresponding lack of restraint on the individual, which
the recognition and acceptance of principles necessarily involves. These facts are patent to all and per-
vade every domain of thought and action.

Such widespread tendencies do not exist without
a cause that can be expressed in as general terms
as the tendencies themselves. So far as I can see
all of these facts have their root in the desire of the
individual of to-day to express himself. The dominant *principle* is that of self-revelation and self-expression. The artist expresses *his* moods; the writer,
his emotions; the pupil, *his* interests; the youth, *his*
own way. None of them, if they are really moderns,
are consciously attempting to express through their
art an everlasting and eternal truth which they recognize as the standard by which they and their work
must be measured. This present situation may well
result from a reaction against the world of fifty or a
hundred years ago. Then our music was written, for
the most part, in regular form. Tennyson was the
great poet; the ladies wore much more comprehensive

apparel; our college course was a rigid requirement
of Greek, Latin, and Mathematics, with a little philosophy and Hebrew; and our manners were mid-
Victorian.

No one can be intimately familiar with the youth
of to-day without realizing the fact that some of
the finest fruits of the spirit are encouraged by this
freedom from restraint and this attempt to express
what is actually felt by the individual. And they are
not the outstanding characteristics of our fathers.
The virtues of frankness, freedom from hypocrisy
and cant, independence, self-reliance, and ambition
are developed in a finer and more vital manner by
our youth of to-day than ever before. Our younger
generation is trying to work out its own life, to express its own thoughts and ambitions as they actually
exist in their own souls rather than under the guidance or suppression of dogmas imposed from the outside. The young man of to-day is content if his
work, or study, contributes to the richness of his own
life and if the product of his effort truly expresses
that life. For he is then in accord with the spirit of
his generation. His struggle is for *freedom* from the
influences that would cramp and dwarf his desires,
his ambitions, and his aspirations. He seeks the
truth, for he feels that the truth shall make him
free. Freedom from the dead hand of dogmatism

and rules, freedom to live his own life, freedom to express his own self truly, is the ambition of our younger generation.

If we stopped here without an attempt to inquire as to whither it is all tending, the picture would be incomplete and not altogether lovely. For the over-powering desire for self-expression is often difficult to distinguish from selfishness, and complete freedom is not unlike chaos and anarchy. For he whose only desire is to find his own life shall lose it. But at the same time there is nothing more certain than that every honest attempt to express the truth that is in one, even if the result does seem erratic and out of line with the conventionality of our fathers, has its value and its effect.

We find the same situation in the physical world. We have learned in recent years that the atom contains a number of so called electrons, which are dart-ing to and fro with almost inconceivable speed and in quite unpredictable directions. The motion of these smallest of particles is called non-coördinated, because it seems to be entirely without relation to any motion of the mass of which they form a part and quite incapable of description in terms of laws or principles. These electrons, as they rush back and forth, are as irresponsible to law and order as any member of the younger generation. Now when a gas

209

like steam is confined in a cylinder, the pressure of steam on the piston is due to the impact of these electrons, which bombard the walls of the cylinder with a perfect fusillade of firing. The higher the temperature of the gas the faster they work. But all in a perfectly haphazard manner so far as the individual particles are concerned. Each electron is expressing itself regardless of any other electron, rushing first in one direction, then in another. But what is the result? Notwithstanding the haphazard way in which the bombardment in the interior of the cylinder seems to be taking place, this bombardment actually makes the piston rod move, and that in accordance with one of the simplest laws of Physics. No man would ever have imagined that the wild and uncoördinated motion of the electrons would ever be brought together so that, irresponsible as each individual is, the result of the whole is team work which not only makes the engine move, but can be expressed so simply that every school boy understands it.

The same God that coördinates the motion of electrons is Lord of the human spirit. All of the erratic and uncoördinated tendencies so prevalent to-day will certainly be synthesized, to the end that order and simplicity will result. This is a statement based on Faith; a Faith that can neither be demonstrated nor argued down.

210

The Younger Generation

There is, however, one great difference between motion in the atom and in our society. We are not electrons. We can help God to do His work of co-ordination. Even if we couldn't He would do it just the same. But it would involve more human suffering and require more time.

What can we do about it? He that findeth his life shall lose it. The man who is seeking merely for self-expression finds that after all he is much more interesting to himself than to anybody else and that the life that he takes so much pains to save is really not worth the trouble if it is taken merely by itself. Just one darting electron more or less is not very significant.

What really great men in the history of our land have sought to save their own lives? Did Washington, did Lincoln, did Lee aim merely at self-expression? They each tried to accomplish the most for their cause. They aimed each day to qualify for the day's responsibilities. To think of Abraham Lincoln or Robert E. Lee as regarding for a moment their own self-development as an end in itself is unthinkable to one who knows their heroic lives. Development of self solely as a means of more effective effort in behalf of some cause greater than one's self is the only kind of self-development that has any place in the life of a real man.

He that loseth his life for my sake shall find it. Just what does that mean here and now? I might enlarge upon the sympathetic and unselfish relation that ought to exist in every family, where the older as well as the younger generation seeks not to dominate, but to contribute to an atmosphere of sweet reasonableness in which each individual *finds* a life of influence and affection by losing it in the common life of the family. I might show how the man on any team or in any coöperative enterprise counts for something only in so far as he places his own success second to that of the group with which he is allied.

I wish rather to indicate the relation of this theme to our attitude toward the laws of the land. The word is on every one's lips that we are living in an age of contempt for law. But our indifference to statutory law is only one phase of the situation. It has already been observed that we are just as lawless in music, philosophy, and manners as we are in our capacity of citizens. One cannot lay any great share of the blame for our disregard for all law on the failure of the community to observe one particular law. To be sure the process that we observe in the attitude of one individual toward statutory law is a cumulative one. To feel a lack of restraint leads us to break a law; the breaking of a law increases our lack of restraint and so we go on. But to assert that the fundamental trouble arises from our restlessness under any one law is like saying that the waving of the branches of the trees makes the wind blow. The difficulty is much deeper and more fundamental than any one law, and unless we regain our spirit of team play and each think less of enjoying our own lives and more of the common good we shall lose what we are short-sightedly struggling to save.

In this nation we pride ourselves on our democracy. This means majority rule. No one ever claimed that the majority is always or necessarily ever right. But the way we have agreed to get things done is to follow laws which the majority agrees upon. If one does not like the result it is his duty as a citizen to do his utmost to convince some of the majority that they are wrong. But in the meantime the ideal citizen obeys the law of which he does not approve. As a last appeal when everything else fails recourse to the right of revolution may be necessary. This country would never have broken from the mother country unless we had decided that repeal was hopeless and revolution the only way of escape.

At the present time, however, we are in the gravest danger of unconsciously bringing about a revolution of which few of us would approve or desire. Each of us is trying to live as a law unto himself, to have his own way, to save his own life and let everything else take care of itself. The very existence not only of our government, but of the democratic form of government, depends upon the acceptance by the community of the decisions of the majority and of securing the modification of laws that are unwise not by breaking them or encouraging others to break them, but by attempting to convert the minority into a majority. Nothing can be clearer than that unless we are willing to lose our own lives, temporarily at any rate, and to accept the principles of following the agreements reached by the majority, our democratic institutions are doomed.

Right here is the danger that besets the youth of to-day. Just as our fathers with their dogmatism and rules ran the risk of a rigid and uncompromising attitude, of hypocrisy and intolerance, so to-day we are in danger of selfish disregard of the welfare of others and a chaotic breaking down of our institutions and governments.

I do not yield to any one in my faith and confidence in the younger generation. Although they are caught in this whirlwind of unrestraint they are honest, more honest than their fathers, and they are seeking to discover the fundamental verities. Although they seem to be seeking to save their own lives, I firmly believe that as many of them are ready to throw themselves into the struggle for the cause of Righteousness as they were in 1917 and to lose themselves in behalf of the common good if they only see it. If they can recognize the direction which the uncoordinated motions of our restless activities is destined to follow, our youth will respond. What can they take as their guide? There is only one adequate guide.

"He that loseth his life for my sake shall find it."

"And whosoever shall be chief among you let him be your servant."

"If thy brother shall trespass against thee, go and tell him his fault between thee and him alone; if he shall hear thee, thou hast gained thy brother."

"And he answered them, saying, Who is my mother or my brethren? And he looked round on them which sat about him, and said, Behold my mother and my brethren."

"Thou shalt love the Lord thy God with all thy heart, and with all thy soul, and with all thy mind, and with all thy strength." This is the first commandment, and the second is like it, namely this: "Thou shalt love thy neighbor as thyself." There is no other commandment greater than these.

THE SUPREME LOYALTY

How deeply the World War left its mark upon the Christian mind of our generation only the Searcher of human hearts will ever know, much less record. But it needed no divination to detect its profound—almost shattering—impact upon the younger men of the pulpit, among whom Dr. Tittle is one of the most gifted. An Ohio man, educated at Ohio Wesleyan University and Drew Theological Seminary, the War found him the brilliant and beloved pastor of the Broad Street Methodist Church, Columbus. He spent two months in the army camps at home and six months at the front, taking part in the St. Mihiel offensive, where he saw what war is when stripped of fine phrases and "the dream those drummers make." When he preached for me in the City Temple in London there were those who felt in his words—vivid, searching, appealing, and still remembered—the ache of a heart well-nigh broken. One hears an echo of the same note in his lectures on *What Must the Church do to be Saved?* with their portrayal of the ghastly deficit between the impotence of organized religion and the appalling need of the time. Such is the background—remote, but still visible—of the sermon here to be read, dealing with the tragedy of clashing loyalties, which speaks for a goodly company of elect youth—not all of them pacifists—in whom nationalism is in conflict with the universalism of Jesus. As a statement of the supreme spiritual loyalty and a plea for a tolerant and free discussion of lesser obligations, it is a notable utterance—at once a torch and a token of the times.

THE SUPREME LOYALTY

ERNEST E. TITTLE, D.D.

FIRST METHODIST CHURCH, EVANSTON, ILL.

"He that loveth father or mother more than me is not worthy of me; and he that loveth son or daughter more than me is not worthy of me." Matt. 10: 37.

I

To the question, What is your supreme loyalty? there is, I venture to think, only one answer which those of us who are gathered here this morning would be willing to give. One after another, would we not promptly and unequivocally answer, My supreme loyalty is to Jesus Christ?

This answer would be given by those among us whose faith in Christ rests upon the authority of the holy catholic church with its nineteen centuries of persistent witness to the lordship of Jesus. And it would be given with equal fervor by those of us whose faith in Christ rests upon the conviction that the accumulating experience of mankind has proved that Jesus is, indeed, the Lord of life. We verily believe that only in him is there fullness of life for the individual or for the world.

219

Ernest E. Tittle, D.D.

And so we are ready this morning to pledge our supreme allegiance to Jesus Christ. In answer to the question, "Do you confess Him as your Lord and Master?" we would say, as one of our number actually did say a few minutes ago, "I do." Some of us might say it with a certain lightness of heart. Others might say it with a very considerable searching of heart. Some of us might say it without thinking through the implications of our avowal. Others might say it with a fairly clear notion of the possible costliness of such an avowal. But to hundreds of us there would seem to be no other possible answer that we could bring ourselves to make. We cannot but repeat after Jesus himself that searching saying, "He that loveth father or mother more than me is not worthy of me; and he that loveth son or daughter more than me is not worthy of me." Nor can we fail to see that although, in this saying, only two great human relationships are mentioned, others are implied. He, for instance, that loveth his university more than Christ is not worthy of Christ. He that loveth his country more than Christ is not worthy of Christ. Are not these admissions also involved? And who among us would hesitate to make them?

When Jesus said, "He that loveth father or mother more than me is not worthy of me," he was, of course, thinking of himself not merely as a human individual,

220

but as a spiritual symbol of the kingdom of God. Supreme loyalty to him meant supreme loyalty to the kingdom of God in heaven and on earth. And let us keep steadily before us the important fact that *when a man pledges supreme loyalty to the kingdom of God, far from surrendering any lesser loyalty, he glorifies every other loyalty.*

When, for instance, a man takes the position that his supreme loyalty is not to his wife nor to his children, but to Jesus Christ, does his family lose by such an allegiance? Does it not rather gain by it all those splendid spiritual values which, down the centuries, have made every truly Christian home a place of refuge and of inspiration? John Bunyan went to jail rather than be untrue to his conscience. He did not enjoy the thought of going to jail. He said, "The parting of my wife and poor children hath often been to me in this place as the pulling of flesh off my bones." One of his children was blind; and he said that the thought of the hardships this poor blind one might be called upon to undergo almost broke his heart to pieces. Yet, in loyalty to his convictions, he remained in Bedford jail twelve years. Did his family suffer by reason of his supreme allegiance to Christ? In one sense, Yes. But only in the sense of physical hardship; only in the sense of physical separation. Never in the sense of spiritual tragedy;

221

never in the sense of spiritual separation. *And in respect of all those noble spiritual loyalties which bind one human soul to other human souls until death, and beyond death, and which dignify and glorify domestic relationships, the Bunyan family gained by this supreme allegiance to Christ.*

Did the family as an institution suffer by reason of this one man's decision to go to jail rather than be untrue to his own conscience? Were any divorces occasioned by it? Were husbands who learned of John Bunyan's incarceration for conscience' sake tempted by reason of it to be disloyal to their wives? Were fathers who heard of his courageous stand for principle led by reason of it to neglect their children? Did any single home in England suffer spiritual shipwreck because of John Bunyan's action? Has not every home in the Anglo-Saxon world in which *Pilgrim's Progress* has been read and reread as a religious classic been brought into a surer cohesion by reason of its author's supreme allegiance to Christ?

When a student takes the position that his supreme loyalty is not to his university, but to Jesus Christ, does his university lose by such an allegiance? Does it lose any great intellectual or spiritual value for which a university is supposed to stand? Financial support it may lose. But what shall it profit a university if it gain millions for buildings or for endow-

The Supreme Loyalty

ment, and lose its own soul—its opportunity for real intellectual leadership? Popular approval it may lose. But if a university, even in the face of popular passion—the spirit of the mob—may not maintain freedom of discussion and freedom of conscience, what moral right has it to live? *No, when a student takes the position that his supreme loyalty must be loyalty to some high and challenging ideal, his university gains in respect of all those truly cultural values which universities exist to foster.*

And when some patriot takes the position that his supreme loyalty is not to his country, but to Jesus Christ, does his country suffer by such an allegiance? Only the unthinking man will ever say that it does.

"He who loves not his home and country which he has seen, how can he love humanity in general which he has not seen?" So asks Dean Inge. And he adds: "There are, after all, few emotions of which one has less reason to be ashamed than the little lump which the Englishman feels when he first catches sight of the white cliffs of Dover." A statement which you and I, applauding, might amend so as to read —"which the returning American feels when he first catches sight of the Statue of Liberty."

When some man expresses a chivalric concern for the welfare of women, we are entitled to know how great is his devotion to that particular woman who

223

has taken him for better, for worse, for richer, for poorer, in sickness and in health till death do them part. And when some man expresses a comprehensive concern for the welfare of mankind, we are entitled to know how much he is doing for that particular portion of mankind which constitutes the community in which he lives.

But if it does not follow that because a man's supreme allegiance is to Jesus Christ, his own family through him is going to suffer, neither does it follow that because a man's supreme allegiance is to the kingdom of God his own country through him is going to suffer. The supreme allegiance of Socrates was not to Athens, but to truth; wherefore, he insisted, his fellow-citizens, instead of punishing him, ought to maintain him at public expense.

How utterly superficial the notion that in order to be loyal to her husband a wife must endorse everything her husband says or does! Must she not sometimes, if she is to be truly loyal to him, take exception to what he says, and disapprove of what he does? And is not equally superficial the notion that in order to be loyal to one's country one must endorse everything that one's country has ever done, is doing, or contemplates doing? Was either Ulysses S. Grant or Abraham Lincoln disloyal to his country when he condemned our war with Mexico? Was

The Supreme Loyalty

Lloyd George disloyal to his country when he condemned, in the very midst of it, her war with South Africa? Was Carl Liebnecht disloyal to his country when he condemned the invasion of Belgium, and the whole position of Germany's militaristic and imperialistic group?

When some man takes the position that loyalty to country involves unquestioning approval of everything that his country does, does he not take a position in which he is utterly powerless to save his country from policies that have in them the seeds of disaster? If a man really loves his country, if he sincerely desires his country's welfare, must he not take the position that his supreme loyalty is not to country, but to Christ—to truth, to justice, to humanity, to God? *As each Sunday morning, on every battleship in the United States navy, above even that dear flag which symbolizes native land, there is hoisted that white flag which symbolizes the kingdom of God, must not every truly loyal American, in his own soul, place the white flag above every other?*

From any man who does take that position, what has his country to fear? Is he the kind of man who goes profiteering in war time? Is he the kind of man who puts rotten leather in shoes that are to be worn by soldiers? Is he the kind of man who is willing to misrepresent the amount of income tax he owes to his government? Is he the kind of man who in Washington, to-day, would be suspected by anybody to be involved in an oil scandal? Or a fight-film scandal? Or a veteran's bureau scandal? Or any other kind of scandal? Men who swear allegiance to high ideals are not always wise. Their judgment, I mean, is not always faultless. But, when all is said, are they the men of whom their country has reason to feel afraid? Are not they just the men on whom their country may confidently rely?

He who loves his father or mother more than Christ is not only unworthy of Christ, he is unworthy of his father and mother. He who loves his university more than Christ is not only unworthy of Christ, he is unworthy of his university. He who loves his country more than Christ is not only unworthy of Christ, he is unworthy of his country. *The higher loyalty, far from betraying the lesser loyalty, is the one thing in all the world that can guarantee the lesser loyalty!*

II

But now, having stressed this fact, I must, in all candor, call attention to another fact—for increasing numbers of persons a peculiarly torturing fact—namely, that the higher loyalty and the lesser loyal-

226

ties do sometimes seem to clash. I have said that to the question, "Do you confess Christ as your Lord and Master?" we who are gathered here this morning would feel that there is for us but one answer—"I do." In our heart of hearts we really want to be supremely loyal to Jesus Christ. But we are dwelling in the midst of a civilization that is semi-pagan. We live and move and have our being in a world that does not, on the whole, accept, much less practise, the principles of Jesus. We are citizens of a state that is less than Christian. *How, then, is it going to be possible for us to discharge the duties of citizenship in a less than Christian state; to live and labor in a world where hideously unchristian deeds are not only done but commanded; to dwell in the midst of a semi-pagan civilization, and maintain, through everything, our loyalty to Christ?*

That is the question which confronts many a modern business man who deep down in his heart endorses, and enthusiastically applauds, the ethical teachings of Jesus, but who, each Monday morning, as he returns to his office, finds it immensely difficult to apply them. He holds, let us suppose, a subordinate position in some large mercantile or manufacturing establishment. And every once in a while he is asked to do, or at least to approve, something which he simply cannot reconcile with the teachings of

Jesus. But how, oh, how shall he solve his moral problem? If he gives up this position, where will he go to find another position in which he may be free to hold fast his allegiance to Christ?

This moral problem becomes excruciatingly difficult when a Christian is ordered by a less than Christian state, in a semi-pagan world, to take up arms against his fellows. I do not happen to know anything about the officer in charge of the submarine which discharged the torpedo that sank the "Lusitania." But let us just suppose this morning that in his heart of hearts he wanted to be loyal to Jesus Christ. He received an order from his government to sink a ship carrying munitions—and women and children. What should he have done? In time of war, a man who really desires to be loyal to Jesus Christ may be ordered to bomb a city, or to explode poison gas shells over it, or to foul its water supply, or to cut off its food supply, or (it is now hinted) to release disease germs in it, or in some other fiendish way to inflict suffering, not only upon men, but upon women and children. What, under such circumstances, should a Christian do? When Christ says, "Treat every man as a brother," and the state says, "Treat certain men as your enemies"; when Christ says, "Maintain toward every man an attitude of good-will," and the state says that good-will to-

228

ward enemies is not permissible, what should a Christian do?

Now this, I think, is a question which every modern disciple of Jesus ought to be putting to his own soul. It is a question which, in my judgment, cannot longer be evaded. And it is a question which every follower of Christ will have to answer for himself. You cannot answer it for me. I cannot answer it for you. No man may answer it for his brother. If some disciple of Jesus comes to the conclusion that, in the event of another war, there is but one thing for him to do, and that is to serve his country by bearing arms, it is not for me, or for any other man, to say to him that in that case he will cease to be a Christian. And if some disciple of Jesus comes to the conclusion that, in the event of another war, he must, in some way, serve his country, but that he cannot, under any circumstances, consent to bear arms, to kill, to inflict suffering upon women and children, it is not for me, or for any man, to say to him that, in that case, he will cease to be a Christian.

Certainly, let me add, *it is not for the Christian church to discourage any of her sons or daughters who are making earnest, and even agonizing, efforts to be loyal to Jesus Christ.* Whatever attitude the state may feel obliged to take toward the "conscien-

Ernest E. Tittle, D.D.

tious objector," the Christian church ought not to make more difficult his already terribly difficult path. If the state decides that in the interest of public safety he should be sent to jail, the church cannot keep him out; but the church can, and should, let him feel that he possesses her profoundest respect for his brave allegiance to what seems to him to be the command of Christ.

As for the church herself, I, for my part, feel very sure that she ought never again, in her official capacity, to bless war. She cannot dictate to her sons and daughters how they shall solve their moral problem. She must not, in my judgment, attempt to legislate in respect of a matter which concerns so vitally the individual conscience. But this one thing she may do. *She may refuse to call holy that which is hideous. She may refuse to call right that which is wrong.* She may humbly confess her own share of the awful failure to prevent war. But by what kind of moral hocus-pocus may she justify her shame? Let the church never assume a holier than thou attitude. But, in the name of truth, let her never again say that black is white. And, in the name of Christ, let her never again officially participate in an orgy of killing and hate. *Let her keep herself in some truly and nobly Christian sense "above the battle"—above the massacre and the madness—so that anguished*

230

*men and women on both sides of the conflict may
know that there is, in a mad-house world, at least one
great organization that is keeping sane and calm
and kind and Christ-like; and by that knowledge be
comforted and sustained and filled with hope.*

If, in the event of another war, the church should
maintain an attitude such as this, is it not at least
possible that, at the close of the war, she could influence, for the good of all, the terms of peace?

III

There is, I think, still another fact to which attention needs to be called. I have said that the problem
presented at this present time to a thoroughly Christian conscience is a truly terrible one. I have said
that it is a problem which each disciple of Jesus must
solve for himself. Now let me suggest that in order
that he may have a fair chance to solve it; in order,
indeed, that the whole world may have a fair chance
to find some way out of the awful situation which
now confronts it, *there must be full freedom of discussion even in respect to the moral legitimacy of
existing laws of the land.* So long as any law stands,
he who violates it must be prepared to pay the pen-
alty. But to take the position that, once a law has
been passed, it is not permissible even to question

Ernest E. Tittle, D.D.

its moral legitimacy, is to take a position which, if it could be maintained, would stop moral progress forever.

Fortunately, for those of us who live in America, the very constitution of our government guarantees freedom of discussion. Its first amendment reads: "Congress shall make no law respecting an establishment of religion or prohibiting the free exercise thereof; or abridging the freedom of speech, or of the press; or the right of the people peaceably to assemble, and to petition the government for a redress of grievances." *How very inconsistent the position of persons who demand a one hundred percent loyalty to the constitution of the United States and then try to limit freedom of discussion!*

But quite apart from this constitutional guarantee, would it not be a bad day for America if the state should attempt to dictate to its teachers what they shall teach, or to its preachers what they shall preach? Would not such a situation prove as intolerable in America as it proved in Russia and in Germany? Would it not turn out to be as dangerous for America as it was for Russia and for Germany?

If the universities of America ever turn over their intellects into the keeping of the state, they will be as powerless to guide the people of America as were the universities of Germany to guide the people of

232

Germany. If the churches of America ever turn over their consciences into the keeping of the state, they will be as powerless to save the people of America as were the churches of Germany to save the people of Germany. During the war, and immediately after it, how many times we put the question: "Why did not the people of Germany rise up against their military masters?" But is it not the answer to this question just the very significant fact that the people of Germany were kept in ignorance by their masters; that they were denied by their masters any chance either to know, or to discuss, political truth? *God forbid that America should ever adopt those methods of terrorism and of oppression which drove Germany into ruin such as has befallen no other nation in modern times.*

I remember hearing one of my professors in the theological school relate an experience which he had in Germany about twenty years ago. He had made some remark a bit derogatory to the Kaiser. His remark was overheard and reported to the police. A kind friend gave him a tip that he was about to be arrested. He took the next train to the coast, crossed the channel, hurried up to London, and went to Hyde Park, where, as he said, he might "cuss" the king to his heart's content. I used to tell this story during the war in order to illustrate the difference be-

233

tween the German method and the British method. I believed then, and I believe now, that the British method was far, far better than the German method. In England, for generations, men have claimed and exercised freedom of discussion. Has freedom of discussion made England weak? No, *freedom of discussion has made the English government one of the strongest and most stable governments in all the world*. Think of a nation passing from a tory government to a labor government without a financial crash!

And now, are we Americans, at this late hour, going to adopt the discredited and discarded German method? We who sing

> My country, 'tis of thee,
> Sweet land of liberty?

Are we going to renounce our political heritage? Are we going to repudiate our own political history? Are we going to say, "Our fathers brought forth upon this continent a new nation, conceived in liberty"; but we, their sons, have become afraid of liberty?

"With a great sum," said a Roman freedman, to a Christian missionary, "obtained I this freedom." And the missionary proudly replied, "But I am free born." With a great sum our fathers obtained "this freedom" which we, free-born Americans, up until

234

now have enjoyed. Back of the American Revolution is the English Revolution. And back of the English Revolution is that great charter, a copy of which may be seen to-day in the British Museum, "injured by age and fire, but with the royal seal still hanging from the shriveled parchment"—that Magna Charta of Anglo-Saxon liberties. With a great sum obtained they this freedom—John Eliot, John Hampton, John Pym, John Hancock, George Washington, Benjamin Franklin, Alexander Hamilton, Thomas Jefferson. May God forbid that now, in days of passion and panic, we should throw away so great and precious and costly a heritage. *Freedom of discussion we must claim and exercise if either as individuals, or as a nation, we are to have any real chance to solve our most momentous problems.*

And now, for one brief, closing moment let us return to the thought with which we started, that our supreme loyalty is to Jesus Christ. If our profession of Christianity amounts to anything, each of us in his own way, but each of us in some way, must strive to crown him Lord of all. It is hardly to be expected that we shall all choose the same way of trying to rid the world of its greatest existing curse—the curse of war and of the whole war system. But, in Christ's name, let us choose some way! How dare we, as Christians, remain passive while forces are generating to hurl the world into another catastrophe unimaginably awful? How dare we let governments blunder along into another abyss through lack of moral initiative? Is it not for Christians, of all people, to furnish moral initiative? To take with respect to war a position *in advance* of the average conscience, and then by unsleeping educational effort bring the long-suffering, because uninformed, masses of mankind to the point where they will demand that war be placed in the same category with dueling, piracy, and slavery?

Then, but not until then, will loyalty to Christ no longer clash with loyalty to Cæsar. For then church and state will together stand at the feet of Jesus and crown him Lord of all.

THE SOURCES OF SURPLUS POWER
IN HUMAN LIFE

Mr. Gilkey was born in Watertown, Mass., in 1889, graduated from Harvard, and after studying in the Universities of Berlin and Marburg, took his theological training at Union Seminary, New York. Ordained to the Presbyterian ministry in 1916, he served for one year as assistant minister of Bryn Mawr Church, and since 1917 has been pastor of the South Congregational Church, Springfield, Mass. He directs an elaborate program of institutional work, and has introduced the motion picture as a definite part of his educational plan. As college preacher at Harvard, Princeton, Chicago, and New York, he is both attractive and effective. The present sermon is typical of the effort of our younger preachers to apply the findings of psychology in helping restless and distracted men and women to discover, develop, and employ spiritual energies in daily life, thereby realizing personal efficiency through religious experience. It is a lesson in spiritual hygiene, and if there had been more preaching of a sort similar some of the popular cults of the day would never have come into being.

THE SOURCES OF SURPLUS POWER IN HUMAN LIFE

JAMES GORDON GILKEY

SOUTH CONGREGATIONAL CHURCH, SPRINGFIELD, MASS.

"I am come that they might have life . . . more abundantly." John 10: 10.

One of the great figures in the rescue mission work of recent years was S. H. Hadley. The story of his own deliverance from the drink habit has been quoted frequently by psychologists. "One Tuesday I was sitting in a saloon in Harlem, a homeless, friendless, dying drunkard. I had pawned or sold everything that would bring a drink. I had not eaten for days, and for four nights I had suffered with delirium tremens from midnight till morning. I had often said: 'I will never be a tramp. I will never be cornered. When the time comes I will find a home in the bottom of the river.' But when the time did come, I was not able to walk a quarter of the way there. . . . Toward evening it came into my head to go to the Jerry McAuley Mission. The place was packed, and it was with difficulty that I made my way to the space near the platform. McAuley rose and told

239

his experience. I found myself saying: 'I wonder if God can save me?' Then I listened to the testimony of twenty or thirty other people, every one of them saved from rum. I made up my mind that I would be saved too, or die right there. When the invitation was given I knelt down with a crowd of drunkards. What a conflict was going on for my poor soul! Something within me said, 'Come!' Something else said, 'Be careful!' I hesitated a moment, and then with a breaking heart I cried: 'Dear Jesus, can you save me?' Never can I describe what happened. Up to that moment I had been filled with utter darkness. Now the brightness of noonday seemed to stream around me. I was a free man again. From that moment I have never wanted a drink of whiskey, and I have never seen money enough to make me take one."

What had happened to that man? Before that moment in the Mission he was enslaved and beaten. After that moment he was free and victorious. Why was he suddenly able to do the thing he had never been able to do before? Most of us would probably agree on this answer. Somewhere or other Hadley had found a new source of power. It was great enough to resurrect his buried self, and keep that buried self—his better self—permanently dominant. Call that new source of power what you will. The fact was that Hadley had stumbled upon it, and in a moment it changed his whole life.

This is no isolated instance. All through history and everywhere about us to-day you find people who have had this experience in one form or another. Some of these people had, like Hadley, been fighting the coarsest of human vices for years. Some of them were of a wholly different type. Living for a long time on a relatively high level of character and achievement, they were suddenly lifted to new heights of power. In essence the experience of all these people is similar. Up to a certain moment their range of action is relatively small. Then comes an instant of psychological release, personal emancipation, spiritual re-birth—call it what you will. And the next moment these people find themselves doing what had hitherto been impossible. Take this incident from a recent English biography. The background is entirely different from that of Hadley's life, but the experience of feeling a sudden access of power is essentially the same. "We both were awakened early in the morning by a cry of pain, sharp and insufferable. We knew whose voice it was, and we ran down the hall to the little parlor at the left. Father was standing there—his hands clenched in his black hair, his eyes full of misery and amazement, his face white as that of the dead. He frightened us. He saw this, or else his intense will mastered his agony. Taking his hands from his head he said slowly and gently, 'Let us give thanks.' He turned to a little sofa in the room. There lay our mother, dead." Where did that sudden self-mastery come from? What was the power that enabled that man to regain composure and face the tragedy with incredible poise? The answer is the one we suggested a moment ago. Men stumble on new sources of spiritual power, and then find themselves doing what seemed—five minutes before—impossible.

I

What are these sources of surplus power? Can they be found and used by ordinary people and under normal circumstances? In recent years scientists have been studying this problem as it has never been studied before. They have begun to reach conclusions which are of the utmost importance to Christianity. For these conclusions are opening before us a new hope—the hope that we shall be able some day to remake human personalities as we have already succeeded in remaking parts of the physical universe. We are now sure that there are at least two sources of surplus power in human life, utilized blindly by the men of the past and waiting to be

242

utilized intelligently by the men of the present. Suppose this morning we consider what these two sources of surplus power are and discuss what we now know about using them.

The first source of surplus power in your life is your own hidden self. Recently a British neurologist made an interesting experiment on three young men in the hope of determining the range—above as well as below normal—of their physical strength. These men took the conventional series of tests, and their strength—under normal circumstances—was carefully noted. Then they were hypnotized, told repeatedly that they were physical weaklings, and put through the tests again. To every one's surprise, their strength dropped to only 30% of normal. Then, still under hypnosis, they were told that they possessed unlimited power. Over and over again this suggestion was made to them, while they went through the tests for the third time. It was startling to find that their strength not only went back to normal, but actually rose to 140% of normal. They were more than a third stronger than they had ever been before. Where did that extra 40% of strength come from? Obviously it did not come from outside. There was no outside place from which it could come. It came from somewhere inside—from reserves of power that had been called into final action.

That experiment explains our new conception of human personality. Your self is no sharply defined and rigidly circumscribed thing. Your powers are constantly varying in extent—shrinking under one set of influences and expanding under another. Most of the time you see only part of your potential abilities, as a general on a battlefield sees only part of his army. Off in the distant regions of the personality are your reserves, waiting to be summoned into action. Sudden need, sudden emotion, sudden inspiration, or a summons that you yourself have arranged will bring them streaming out of that hinterland to offer you their surplus energy. We all know from experience how true this is in the matter of physical exertion. In a crisis even a weakling will display the strength of a giant. The same thing is true of your spiritual powers—your endurance, your poise, your ability to achieve. Under normal circumstances you see only part of these powers. The rest are waiting off in the recesses of the self for the summons to action that will bring them scurrying out of the darkness to help you. You question all this? Watch yourself the next time you meet a spiritual emergency! Will you break under the strain, go to pieces, collapse in tears and tremblings? Nothing of the kind! Your reserves will rush forward to save you, just as they did in the case we quoted from the English biography. The extra 40%—spiritual as well as physical. And it exists in every one of us. Rufus Jones writes: "There are within reach of us all vast reservoirs of spiritual energy, if we only knew how to tap them. There are great stores of power, if we could only find the key. Happy are the men and women who, at the critical moments of life, succeed in breaking through the walls within themselves and gaining access to these storehouses of surplus energy."

How can we call in these reserves of the self? Recent study has suggested two ways. The first is this: If you want to utilize your reserve powers, you must resolutely sweep from your life the obstacles that block these reserves as they struggle forward to aid you. We see clearly now what some of these inner obstacles—"inhibitions" we call them—are. Fear is one of the worst. If there are great fears and haunting worries in your mind you need never expect to utilize the ultimate spiritual energies of your personality. The energies are there, and they are forever struggling to come to your aid—new courage, surplus hope, extra poise. But your fears and worries barricade them within the recesses of the self. Try as they will, they cannot pass that boundary you have allowed to rise. You doubt all this? Look at the next "worrier" you meet. Does he give the appearance of getting all of himself into action, or only a scant 30%? The sense of guilt is another inner obstacle. We may not be able to explain why, but the experience of ten thousand times ten thousand proves the fact. If a man has done wrong, knows he has done wrong, and is beset day and night by some haunting sense of guilt, he need never expect to swing all his powers into action. He has a divided self—in the foreground a few meager abilities, then the strange barrier his sense of guilt has erected, and behind that all the powers he needs for triumphant living. You question that? See how much fine work you can do, how well you can concentrate all your powers, when you have a guilty conscience. A treasured grudge is perhaps the strangest inner barrier of all. Most of us know from experience what a sense of inner relief comes when we drop an ancient quarrel, forgive and forget, and begin to smile again. Why does the sense of inner relief, relaxed tension, release of power follow so inevitably? Because that grudge had built a barrier across the personality. Part of our spiritual power was imprisoned behind it, pushing and straining to find its normal outlet. Sweep the barrier away, and the self is instantly reunited. The strain vanishes automatically. Here are the conclusions we are reaching to-day, thanks to our new psychological science. Did you ever realize that Jesus sensed these facts centuries ago? Listen. "Be not anxious for the morrow." Why was Jesus so eager to drive fear from human lives? Because He realized that fear divides self, interrupts the normal flow of spiritual power, robs men of their reserves of strength, and finally leaves them weak and beaten. "Blessed are the pure in heart. They shall see God." Why was Jesus so eager to make men cleanse their lives of every taint of sin, every shadow of the sense of guilt? Because He sensed the fact that any consciousness of wrong-doing divides a human life, and robs it of all its surplus power. The more abundant life, with its vivid sense of God, the great gift Jesus had for humanity, is impossible as long as sin piles its bleak wall across the very center of the personality. "Forgive, even until seventy times seven." Why forgive, over and over again? Jesus knew what havoc a grudge works, not only on the persons against whom it is directed, but even more on the person who holds it. We must forgive . . . or the secret wall of hatred shuts from us all the reserves that would change our defeat into victory. Scientific study is proving all this true to-day. Spiritual genius revealed it to Jesus centuries ago.

Here is the other way to call in the reserves of your personality. Believe better things about yourself and your value to the world. Few people realize what a tremendous effect a man's belief about himself exerts on his own inner nature. For centuries men have felt blindly that there was some such connection, and they have formulated such proverbs as "He wins who thinks he can," "According to your faith be it unto you." To-day we are beginning to realize that these vague suppositions are susceptible of laboratory verification. The reiterated suggestion of weakness makes a man believe wretched things about himself, and his strength drops—as the British neurologist proved—to only a fraction of normal. The reiterated suggestion of power makes a man believe fine things about himself, and his strength rises far above normal. Your belief about yourself either holds back or calls in all your reserves of energy. Against the background of such facts, one can discern the real significance of the two views of life we find current in the world to-day. Here is a poet who accepts as true the drab interpretation of existence offered by the materialist.

> A little while when I am gone
> My life will live in music after me,
> As spun foam lifted and borne on
> After the wave is lost in the full sea.
> Awhile these nights and days will burn
> In song, with the brief frailty of foam,
> Living in light before they turn
> Back to the nothingness that is their home.

Sources of Surplus Power in Human Life

Suppose you make that your estimate of your life and your value to the universe. A bit of foam—flung up for a moment as the winds of fate sweep across the surges of inert and purposeless matter. An instant of rainbow radiance—the glory of your ephemeral achievement. Then the foam sinks back forever in the wave, and wind and sea sweep on blindly as before. Suppose you accept as true that interpretation of life and your part in it. You will have a hard time bringing into action your spiritual reserves! Your inner attitude and your belief about yourself are not adequate for the task. It is as though you told the young men in the English laboratory that they were hopeless weaklings, and then expected them to reach the record of 140% in their test. Now take the other interpretation of life, given to the world by Jesus, and dominant in the life and thought of thousands of Christians to-day. Stevenson, waiting for death on his island in the Pacific, phrased it splendidly:

> The embers of the day are red
> Beyond the murky hill:
> The kitchen smokes, the bed
> In the darkling house is spread,
> The great sky darkens overhead,
> And the great woods are shrill. . . .
> So far have I been led,
> Lord, by Thy will;

James Gordon Gilkey

So far have I followed, Lord,
And wondered still.
The breeze from the embalmed land
Blows sudden toward the shore
And claps my cottage door. . . .
I hear the signal, Lord, I understand.
The night at Thy command
Comes.
I will eat and sleep, and will not question more.

See what a contribution Christian faith has to make to your life! Here is this half-discovered personality of yours—part well known, part waiting to be explored and put to use. How can you call into action the reserves of your self, unite everything in your nature for the struggle of the years? Jesus Christ can show you the way. Drop these fears and worries. Sweep away these secret sins. Forgive, as you want God to forgive you. And then accept as true Jesus' interpretation of life. Live on it. Your life—surrounded by the love and the care and purpose of God. Your work—part of an eternal purpose for the world. Your future—safe in the hands of the Most High. Try that way of living, Jesus' way. Do you know what will happen? All the reserves of your personality will be released and surge forward to help you. A psychologist would say you had tapped a new source of power. A poet of long ago put the same truth in the symbolic language of the Orient.

250

Sources of Surplus Power in Human Life

"Jesus said: He that drinketh of the water that I shall give him shall never thirst. For the water that I shall give him shall become in him a well of water, springing up into eternal life. If any man thirst, let him come unto me and drink!"

II

The second source of surplus power in your life lies just beyond your personality, but is forever in contact with it. This second source of power is the thing we call God. How does a modern Christian conceive of God? As you stand before me, I realize there are two distinct parts to you. There is the physical body which I see and touch. It is the most obvious thing about you. But, after all, there is more to you than a body. Permeating every part of your physical organism there is something else, vastly more important. It is unseen, to be sure, but it is indubitably real. Your spirit, soul, personality, life —call it what you will. I cannot localize this second element anywhere in your body. I can only say it permeates every part of you. I find it working through your hands and your mind to create material objects. I hear it revealing its desires through the words you speak. I see it slowly and persistently displaying its own inner nature in the kind of a life it impels you to live. Invisible and intangible—but how real! So real that its disappearance causes the greatest change imaginable in your physical organism. The change we call death. What is true of you as an individual seems equally true of the great universe around us all. The most obvious things in that universe are the physical objects that make their instant appeal to our senses. But the more we think about this universe, the harder it becomes to explain and understand it if we conclude there is nothing here but an indiscriminate welter of objects to be felt and touched and seen. A more reasonable theory is that a World Personality, a Cosmic Soul, a Creative Intelligence permeates it all, just as your tiny personality permeates your little body. We cannot localize this Spirit-of-the-Universe, but day by day we can see this Spirit active about us. Working through the forces of the natural world to create material things. Speaking to us through beauty and inner ideals, through the appeal of the prophet or the cry of suffering humanity. Revealing its own ultimate purpose and nature in the kind of a world which it is slowly creating before the eyes of the generations. This is what a modern Christian believes about God. God is no strange, erratic Being, localized in some isolated and sacred spot, working occasional and monstrous wonders in the physical universe for the benefit of a few favorites. Far from it! He is the Spirit permeating all life, working in us and through us and beyond us to guide and control an ever-evolving world.

> I made a pilgrimage to find the God—
> I listened for His voice at holy tombs,
> Searched for the print of His immortal feet
> In dust of broken altars, yet turned back
> With empty heart. But on the homeward road
> A great light came upon me . . . and I heard
> The God's voice singing in a nesting lark,
> Felt His sweet wonder in a swaying rose,
> Received His blessing from a wayside well,
> Looked on His beauty in a lover's face,
> Saw His bright hand send signals from the sun!

One who grasps this new conception of God will be able to understand why we think of Him as a second source of power in human life. This World-Spirit lies just beyond our tiny human spirits. They open onto Him, as a hundred streams and inlets and bays along the seaboard open onto the vastness of the deep. Press into the depths of your own nature, and the first thing you meet is your own undiscovered self. Press beyond that, past the boundary of individual life, through the doorway that separates your personality from the totality of life, and what do you meet? You meet the beginning of the vastness of God. You say all this is imaginative poetry, religious speculation? Oh, no! Some of the men who have meant most to science have finally made this answer to the riddle of existence. Listen to William James. "Man becomes conscious that his own spiritual life is coterminous with a More of the same quality, which is operative in the universe outside him. He can keep in working touch with it, and in a fashion get on board of it and save his higher life when all his lower being goes to pieces in the wreck." That is the way in which a scientist phrases this great conviction. A religious leader puts the same thought in glowing figures of speech. Dr. Fosdick writes: "Where does the restlessness of April have its source? Every tree in its discontent hastens to make buds into leaves. Every blade of grass is tremulous with impatient life. No tree, however, is a sufficient explanation of its own haste and dissatisfaction. No flower has in itself the secrets of its own eager growth. The Spirit of Life is abroad once more, and crowding itself everywhere on dead forms makes them bloom again. We too are confronted throughout our years with an Eternal Life that strives to express itself through us. We can never escape from this Ever-Present God. Every time we open an inspiring book His spirit is pleading for entrance into our hearts. Every time we pray He stands at the door and knocks. Every time some great cause demanding sacrifice lays its claim upon us, this God is pleading to be let into our lives. Our hunger for food, our love for family and friends are no more direct and tangible and immediate experiences than these dealings with the Eternal Spirit." Sources of surplus power? You have only begun to draw upon them when you utilize what lies within your human self. Beyond your human resources lie the resources of God. As the harbors and inlets merge silently and secretly—somewhere—into the great deep. How much can God do? "My ways are higher than your ways, and my thoughts than your thoughts." The deep stretches out . . . who knows how far?

How can you draw help from God? This is the ultimate question in religion, and Jesus gave a very daring answer. Jesus insisted that we can get God's help without any pleading, any teasing, any bribing through rich gifts or sumptuous offerings or reiterated petitions. If you want God's help all you have to do is start living at your best and ask for it. Instantly God responds—no matter who you are, where you are, what you have been in the past, or what you need for the future. "Every one that asketh receiveth. Every one that seeketh findeth. To every one that knocketh it shall be opened." Have you enough confidence in Jesus to believe Him on that point? If you have, everything in your life will

255

begin to change. You will begin to draw on your own hidden powers. And beyond them on the resources of the Spirit of Life Itself. Here is the good news Jesus tried to bring. We do not have to fight the battle unaided. God is here too, with all His help. Waiting for only one thing. For us to say: "Come!"

> Out of the vastness that is God
> I summon the power to heal me:
> It comes . . . with peace ineffable
> And patience, to anneal me.
> Out of the vastness that is God
> I summon the power to still me:
> It comes . . . from inner depths divine
> With destinies that thrill me.
> Out of the vastness that is God
> I summon the strength to keep me,
> And from all fleshly ills that fret
> With spirit winds to sweep me:
> Ajar I set my soul-doors
> Toward unbounded life . . .
> And lo, infinitudes of power
> Flow through me, vigor-rife!

KNEE-DEEP IN JUNE

Dr. Jenkins was born in Kansas City in 1869, and for many years has been pastor of the Linwood Boulevard Christian Church in his native city, and one of its distinguished citizens. He was educated at Bethany College and Harvard University, and entered the ministry of the Church of the Disciples at Indianapolis. Later he became president of the University of Indianapolis, and still later of Kentucky University. Until recently he held what he called "a double-barreled job" as editor and publisher of the *Kansas City Post,* while still serving a great church. He has published many books of sermons, essays, and stories, such as *The Man in the Street and Religion, The Protestant, Facing the Hindenburg Line,* and *Princess Salome.* He unites in an unusual manner qualities not often found together, the scholar and the orator, the man of affairs and the man of the spirit, the philosopher and the poet. The present sermon shows him dealing with a large theme, using vivid colors with deft stroke, direct in his thought and winning in his appeal—refuting the pessimism and futilitarianism of the day.

KNEE-DEEP IN JUNE

BURRIS A. JENKINS, D.D.

LINWOOD CHRISTIAN CHURCH, KANSAS CITY

"Now learn a parable of the fig tree: When his branch is yet tender, and putteth forth leaves, ye know that summer is nigh: so likewise ye, when ye shall see all these things, know that it is near, even at the doors." Matt. 24: 32, 33.

To-day is the mid-most day of June; and June is the topmost month of the year. On this continent June corresponds to the time when in the East the fig tree has put forth its full and perfect leaf. So when Jesus says in the twenty-fourth of Matthew: "Now from the fig tree learn a parable: when his branches now become tender, and putteth forth leaves, we know that the summer is nigh," He is talking of the season corresponding to mid-June.

James Whitcomb Riley, from whom the title of this sermon is borrowed, has a homely rural poem which goes to the heart of every one reared on a farm on the American Continent.

> Tell you what I like the best—
> 'Long about knee-deep in June,
> 'Bout the time strawberries melts
> On the vines—some afternoon
> Like to jes' git out and rest,
> And not work at nothin' else!

259

Burris A. Jenkins, D.D.

Orchard's where I' ruther be—
Needn't fence it in for me!
  Jes' the whole sky overhead
    And the whole airth underneath—
    Sorto' so's a man kin breathe
  Like he ort, and kindo' has
Elbow-room to keerlessly
    Sprawl out len'thways on the grass—

Then he draws the vivid picture of June on the farm. The bluebird's nest, the old apple tree, swallows skimming and bob-whites whistling, the chicken-hawk high overhead and the hen gathering her brood under her wing. He tells how lazy one can be, with his straw hat across his eyes, peering up through it at the skies with clouds of gold and white and blue. He sums up by declaring that March holds "nothin' new," April's altogether too "brash" for him, and May fickle with its hints of sunshine and a lonely bird or two.

Drap asleep, and it turns in
'For daylight and snows agin!—
But when June comes—Clear my throat
  With wild honey! Rench my hair
In the dew! and hold my coat!
  Whoop out loud! and throw my hat!—
  June wants me, and I'm to spare!
  Spread them shadders anywhere,
  I'll git down and waller there,
    And obleeged to you at that!

Knee-deep in June

The poem is as homespun as Burns. That last stanza holds a thrill as deep, though not so sad, as almost anything in the works of the Scotch plowman poet.

If, however, Riley is not sufficiently dignified and elegant for some minds, then turn to Lowell in the "Vision of Sir Launfal." It seems that only American poets sing the glories of June in this fashion, perhaps because June is, in this land, the most satisfying of all the twelve months.

> And what is so rare as a day in June?
>   Then, if ever, come perfect days;
> Then Heaven tries earth if it be in tune,
>   And over it softly her warm ear lays;
> Whether we look, or whether we listen,
> We hear life murmur, or see it glisten;
> Every clod feels a stir of might,
>   An instinct within it that reaches and towers,
> And, groping blindly above it for light,
>   Climbs to a soul in grass and flowers.

Neither of these poems, nor for the matter of that both of them, go much beyond the little parable of the fig-tree which our Master puts into but a sentence or two. June is the month of leaves, but not of fruit, of foliage, but not yet of harvest. It is the month of hope, expectancy, even assurance, but it is not yet the time of full realization. And this is what Jesus means, it would appear, by His little

261

thumb-nail sketch of the fig tree with its big broad leaves. The promise of the fruit is undoubtedly there, but the ripe figs are not yet ready to gather. Whoever refuses to see in the broad leaves of the fig tree the assurance of the coming fruitage is blind to the signs of the times and loses the brightest anticipation of the year. June is the greenest month. Then the trees are at their best, most gloriously clad, before yet the caterpillars and the blight have begun to get in their work of destruction, and before yet the drouth and blistering heat of mid-summer have shriveled and curled the luxuriant vegetation.

"Now is the winter of our discontent made glorious summer." Now when the wheat is knee-high may we be assured that it will soon be waist-high, turn golden, and, falling before the reaper, lie bound in bundles in long wind-rows. Now do we know that the knee-high corn will soon be above our heads, tasseled, and while rustling and shivering in the hot mid-summer wind, be rapidly ripening to its silken perfection. What does all this mean except a cycle of renewed growth, expansion, development? And what does Jesus mean, except the coming of the Son of Man in a progress that human eyes ought to be able to see and to understand.

No doubt Dean Inge of St. Paul's is entirely correct when he states that such a thing as progress is impossible to conceive when we think of the entire universe. Change, the alteration of atoms, the fusion of star dust, the cooling of worlds, the rise of vegetation and of animal life and then perhaps its gradual extinction on this, that, or the other planet—all this is conceivable, but may or may not be progress. Nevertheless, so far as the human race is concerned—and that after all is the thing in which we are interested—man has got hold of the idea of growth, development, evolution, and the idea has got hold of him. To many minds, like that of G. Stanley Hall, who is typical of hundreds of others, the idea of such an evolution or progress is nothing less than an inspiration which illuminates all the phases of thought. Certainly there can be no shadow of doubt that in all the intellectual life of our day the belief in progress, in an end and aim and purpose in the world and in human affairs, is the touch-stone by which everything is tested.

Jesus seems to put the seal of His approval upon this attitude. He apparently wishes to convey the impression that His coming is not only gradual but perceptible. This is not to say that He anticipates the modern doctrine of evolution. No one can claim that Christ is an evolutionist. Never at any time in His teaching is He concerned with scientific or historical facts. It may be claimed, however, that

263

Burris A. Jenkins, D.D.

His ideas are entirely in harmony with the conception of growth, development, which we have come to term evolution. Moreover St. Paul, in his address at Mars Hill hints at the "increasing purpose" that runs through the affairs of the world and of men. In his epistles, too, more than once he indicates a preparation in history for "the fullness of the times." This is not to claim that Paul was an evolutionist; but it is to claim that sacred scripture has caught fore-gleams of this modern scientific doctrine.

Certain it is that religious teachers of to-day are depriving themselves of a very great source of light and strength if they reject the hypothesis of evolution. It is an extremely convenient and illuminating method of reasoning concerning history and the affairs of humanity, just as well as concerning rocks and animal life. To deny oneself of it is to be thrown back upon such conceptions as that of a visible, corporeal, and sudden second coming of Christ, which He certainly does not teach in such passages as this little parable of the fig tree. He insists that we ought to be able to see the signs of His coming—to read the signs of the times. Of course there are many who have professed to read such signs in wars and rumors of wars; but it seems that like the poor we have these always with us. How much more clarifying it is to our vision to be able to point with certainty to the luxurious June leaves of Christ's visible presence in the affairs of this world as they go forward in a steady stream of development.

To be sure if one insists upon holding that humanity is only about six thousand years old upon this planet, he will not be able to read such signs of the times into the affairs of men. It is to be freely admitted that we have not grown much in six thousand years. The difference between Moses, for example, and George Washington is scarcely appreciable. The contrast between Abraham, the father of the faithful, and Abraham Lincoln, the father of a race of freed men, is not so glaring as to command instant acceptance and appreciation. Perhaps there is not a long step forward from Socrates or Confucius to Emmanuel Kant or William James. Moreover, it is only by humanity and human character that we are to judge progress, not by the things with which man has surrounded himself. It is easy enough to point to steam engines, electric lights, telephones, airplanes, and radio to prove that the world has grown; but when you have pointed to them you have proved nothing. It is only character that counts. You must prove that man has grown and that cannot be proven within the span of six thousand years.

If, however, you are able to admit that man has been upon this planet hundreds of thousands of years or, for aught we know, five hundred million years, then you have something to go on. From the cave man living in the rocks, cowering from the beasts of the forest, just beginning dimly to perceive the value of a club or of a stone in his struggle for life, to the civilized man of to-day living comfortably and safely in artificially heated and cooled houses with a steady and uninterrupted supply of provision and with most of his efforts given to intellectual and even artistic pursuits—this is indeed a far cry. Here is growth beyond all doubt. Here is the luxuriant vegetation of the June of human history. Here are indubitable signs of the times.

> A fire mist and a planet,
> A crystal and a cell,
> A jelly-fish and a saurian,
> And a cave where the cavemen dwell;
> Then a sense of law and of beauty,
> A face turned from the clod;
>   Some call it evolution, and others call it God.

It is quite possible, nevertheless, taking humanity not as individuals but in the large, to observe even in the last two thousand years the growth of the fig tree leaf, the proof of the parable of Christ. As a heritage of the entire race knowledge has grown and is growing greatly. There is much more absorption in things of the mind, which of course means things of the spirit, wherever Christ has gone than there was before He came into the world. And Principal Jacks sees in education almost a religion, for the immediate future.

The other day I was riding all day on a westbound train reading *The Life and Confessions of a Psychologist,* by G. Stanley Hall. In the late afternoon I stepped into the smoking compartment and was soon followed by the Negro porter. Six feet and an inch tall and splendidly proportioned, black as broadcloth, with a little mustache, he stood a moment and then said:

"I'd like to read that book in your berth, sir."

Astonished, I turned on him and began asking him questions.

"Have you read psychology?"

"Yes, sir. Majored in it at the university."

"What university?"

"Howard University, Washington, D. C."

"Did you graduate?"

"Yes, sir. Degree of A.B."

"What are you going to do now?"

"Just waiting to get money enough ahead to go on to medical college."

He went backward under the rapid fire of my questions and sat down, which possibly a porter is not expected to do in the smoking room and in the

presence of "gentlemen." Recognizing him, however, as a brother in the great fraternity of scholars
to which I have long humbly aspired to belong, I
promptly took my seat beside him, and we had a
very pleasant conversation about his prospects.
Surely, though still a hewer of wood and drawer of
water, there is some advance between his ancestry
of a few hundred years ago on the Congo and him.
Here is growth, development, emergence from the
material into the spiritual. And what shall be said
about our own ancestry who within two thousand
years used to drink blood out of skulls and often
freeze to death in the forests of Northern Europe?
Probably most of them died in the thirties and the
forties; and no doubt a man who attained the age
of fifty was an old man indeed. Now we consider
that the ripest and most useful time in man's life
is from forty-five to at least sixty-five. We have
no statistics for more accurate information concerning longevity, so far as our Viking fathers are concerned; but the chances are that the fair-haired
races of to-day average twenty to thirty years more
of life, and that too in the most spiritual period of
life, than did their fathers of two thousand years
ago. Here then is leafage of the spirit, a sign of the
coming of the Son of Man.

In this city lives a man of thirty-five who was

cited by General Pershing in the Château-Thierry sector for making maps of the salient behind the German lines. He was Major Roberts then; he is plain Mr. Roberts now, grubbing with a trowel in the garden of his little home. He made the maps by calculating angles by the stars. Everybody said that it could not be done, but he did the impossible. He has made five thousand such maps, putting in the altitudes of mountains and hills without traveling over the ground. He is just waiting to start next winter with a scientific expedition to the wild heart of North Mongolia to make a map of all that undiscovered country. Just a few days ago he had to cable the British Government refusing to go to the upper waters of the Orinoco upon a similar expedition. He will be in Mongolia from three to five years. Meanwhile, with his wife and baby, he lives in a modest little cottage and grubs in a garden with a hand tool. Is he not almost a million years in advance of King Canute or even Richard of the lion heart? Knowledge is power. Says Tennyson:

> Let knowledge grow from more to more,
>   But more of reverence in us dwell,
>   That mind and soul according well
> May make one music as before,
>   But vaster!

So one might go on citing instances of purely intellectual evolution, but what shall be said about even more spiritual concerns? Man is not afraid of God or the gods as he was two thousand years ago. Man is tentatively beginning to love God and to comprehend that God is not Fear but God is Love. The fig tree leaves of a fuller and richer comprehension of the Almighty and the eternal are growing apace; and the June of man's affection for his Eternal Father is coming on with man's increasing confidence in Christ. We begin to understand that what Christ was that God is.

Such increased sense of the Father of our human family is drawing us closer to each other. We value human life, human welfare, and human happiness far more than we used to do. It is no longer considered just the thing to walk over one another in the gaining of selfish ends and aims. Dimly we are beginning to discern that the same attitudes which we assume in family life we should also put into practice in the larger relationships, social, business, political, and international.

Some thirty years ago or so a senator from Kansas declared that the Golden Rule had no place in business or politics. That senator was retired at the next election, possibly not exclusively for that utterance, but one cannot help believing largely on account of it. It was not that the people of Kansas

were putting the Golden Rule noticeably into politics
or business at that time; but it was because they
had a sneaking notion that they ought to do so;
and they didn't like for their senator to say that it
was impossible. Now all over Kansas and all over
this country Rotary Clubs, Kiwanis Clubs, Coöperative Clubs, and a dozen other varieties of circular
clubs are preaching day in and day out that the
Golden Rule as well as all the other precepts of
Christ are not only ideal but practicable in business
affairs, are indeed the best possible business.

In Cincinnati is the largest clothing manufacturer
perhaps in the world—Arthur Nash. His business
is founded on the Golden Rule. Investigated by the
Federal Council of Churches and by the American
Federation of Labor, there were only a few superficial faults that could be found in his administration.
He never has a strike; his people are part owners
of the concern and are the most highly paid workmen in the garment business. The last time I saw
Arthur Nash, he said to me: "Doctor, my worst fear
is that I shall be a millionaire in spite of myself and
I don't want to be a millionaire." The other day
the papers carried a story to the effect that the Nash
Clothing Company had declared a one hundred percent dividend, and Arthur Nash would have become
a millionaire at once had he not parceled out his

share of the dividend amongst the other employees. Here is the coming of the Son of Man. Have we eyes to read the signs of the times?

Has it ever been your strange experience to sit in a boat before daylight or just at dawn on a mist-beclouded river or ocean and try to locate sounds and voices coming to you over the water? Perhaps you heard the rattle of oars in row-locks or the flapping of sails or the siren of a tug, and yet you could not see a thing; and you had the feeling that you were totally deceived in the direction in which sounds were coming. Mysterious, eerie, altogether fearsome, is such an experience on fog-covered waters. One such morning on the flagship of an American fleet of destroyers out of Brest Harbor we let go a convoy of transports carrying wounded men home and lay by to pick another convoy bringing fresh troops from America. We knew that in that coming convoy, somewhere out there in mid-ocean, was "La France," one of the biggest ships on the seas, and the pride of the French Merchant Marine. How the American sailors ever hoped to sight that convoy in that darkest hour which came just before the dawn, made still darker by the mistiness of the morning, was beyond my comprehension. Yet the commander waved his hand to the shrouds over his head and said: "Listen for that young fellow on the starboard lookout." Sure enough by and by rang out a young voice crying, "Ship ahoy!"

"Where away?"

"Off the starboard bow!"

It was twenty minutes before I could descry at all the black smudges of the convoys on the horizon.

On another morning two thousand years ago a little group of fishing men were out in a boat in the misty darkness. Not only was the surface of the water dark, but the horizons of their hearts were black with hopelessness and despair. Nearly three years they had pinned their faith and all their earthly hope to One who had just died ignominiously the death of a felon on a cross. A man had buried him and Rome had put a seal on his tomb. All the hope of these fishermen now lay shattered and their dreams of a kingdom were only fragments and shards. One said: "I go a-fishing." And they all went. Suddenly out of the darkness, out of the mists and blackness in their souls, there loomed a presence. It was their very Lord, risen and come back to them. They said afterwards that He walked to them on the water. No wonder they thought so. Something turned them from darkness to hope, from the blackness of night to the dawn of even a greater day than they had ever dreamed. Beside this a mere walking on water by a man is an insignificant occurrence.

Burris A. Jenkins, D.D.

From this time forward Christ walked on the tide
of all their life, as He has walked steadily forward
on all the rivers, lakes, and oceans of the world.
He said He would come a second time and He has
already come. He is constantly coming with a wonderful and beautiful evolution, yes, even a revolution
in the thoughts of men, in the lives of men, in the
spirits of men. Can we not see him coming in the
glory of the June morning and do our hearts not
leap up to meet him?

THE REALISM AND IDEALISM OF LIFE

Swing, Hillis, Gunsaulus—it is a shining tradition in which Dr. Shannon stands in the pulpit of Central Church, Chicago; and he ably maintains it by virtue of qualities akin to those of his predecessors, as well as by an insight and art all his own, speaking to a goodly company in Orchestra Hall, and an enormous radio audience besides. Born on a farm in Kansas, educated in Webb School, Bell Buckle, Tenn., and at Harvard University, Dr. Shannon entered the Methodist ministry in 1889, his chief pastorate being at Grace Church, Brooklyn. Six years later he became pastor of the Reformed Church on Brooklyn Heights, and went to Chicago in 1920. An outstanding figure among the younger men of the American pulpit, he may be said to belong to the Gunsaulus-Hillis school of preaching—picturesque, imaginative, richly rhetorical, at times gorgeously colorful. In his earlier books, such as *The Soul's Atlas* and *The Enchanted Universe*, his fancy sometimes ran riot in a tropical profusion of imagery: if in his later sermons, like *The Economic Eden* or *The Infinite Artist*, it is more subdued and disciplined, it is only the decorative exuberance with which an authentic messenger clothes a penetrating insight into spiritual reality and the problems of human life and destiny. Dr. Shannon is now in the full tide of a ministry in which men of every faith have a right to an honorable pride and promise.

THE REALISM AND IDEALISM OF LIFE

FREDERICK F. SHANNON

CENTRAL CHURCH, CHICAGO

"My God, my God, why hast thou forsaken me?" Matt.
27: 46.
*"Go unto my brethren and say to them, I ascend unto my
Father and your Father, and my God and your God."* John
20: 17.

My subject is the realism and idealism of life,
as interpreted by the words and experience of the
Lord Christ. Our first text is shot through with
such solemnity that one hesitates to pronounce it.
It appears originally in the Twenty-second Psalm,
which contains, according to Tertullian, "the whole
Passion of Christ." Yet, uttered by our Lord in
His dying hour, the words are invested with a hush
of wonder and majesty which cause sensitive souls
to repeat them with becoming reluctance. They
seem to voice what we may venture to call the
realism of life. The second text are the words of
the Master to Mary Magdalene in the Garden on
that first Easter morning. By way of contrast, and
in the light of Christ's triumph over sin, death, and
the grave, they define, in a large and glorious fashion,

277

the idealism of life. At any rate, setting the two passages with their unfathomable experiences together, we have what I like to call: The story of the God-Man against the universe, and of His final vindication by the universe which apparently forsook Him.

I

Consider the realism of life. "My God, My God, why hast Thou forsaken Me?" Here is realism indeed—realism drenched with the darkest rain that ever fell from life's midnight skies. More terrible than philosophic pessimism, more awful than scientific agnosticism, more oppressive than all skeptical speculations whatsoever, this experience of the profoundest Soul ever housed in flesh bids one pause and ponder. I can endure Omar's cynicism, and Nietzsche's ravings, and Schopenhauer's despair. Each saw only a fragment of life and misinterpreted even that. But what shall we say in the presence of the sanest, deepest, wisest, and best, when He, too, seemingly finds a universe bereft of its God? This, surely, is enough to make one shudder. This, I say, is the climax of despair, but it is not all there is. Other factors are present also. Before the climax can be fully appreciated, these must be adequately weighed.

The Realism and Idealism of Life

Jesus was forsaken by His friends. Let us confess that the way Jesus wooed and won those fishermen and artisans is one of the supreme romances of the soul. He found them dull, unresponsive, disregarded by the social circles of the period. But behold Him working them over! No sculptor ever gave such attention to his marble; no painter ever dreamed of his canvas; no poet ever brooded over his songs; no architect ever studied his designs; no gardener ever caressed his flowers; no young mother ever leaned over the face of her sleeping babe—none ever gave his being to matter or mind as Jesus gave Himself to those first disciples. Little by little did they realize and own His irresistible spell. As the buried root finally signals to the sun with banners of beauty, so, at last, did James and John and Peter and the others come forth from their dungeons of flesh and view the mountains of divine grandeur towering above them in the Christ of God.

And Peter! Why, did not Peter—the imperfect and the impetuous—feel the quickening tides of heroism run so deep and strong in his soul that, when the Master suggested they would all be offended in Him—did not Peter declare: "Even if I must die with Thee, yet will I not deny Thee"? Oh, Peter, what a human brother you are—bone of our bone, flesh of our flesh! A few hours later when Peter, James, and John are told off by the Master to be nearest Him in His agony, they are one and all overcome, not by death, but by sleep! Moreover, when the mob, guided by Judas, comes to take the Master in the garden, we read: "Then all the disciples forsook Him and fled." Jesus was forsaken by His friends; even the inner circle melted away before the raging fires of iniquity that swept the olive orchard through!

Jesus was forsaken by Religion. "Now the chief priests and the whole council sought false witnesses against Jesus, that they might put Him to death." Talk about realism! If you care to see realism in its blackest expression, realism uttering itself in unspeakable diabolism, I commend to you that ex-chief priest, Annas, and his crafty son-in-law, Caiaphas, the reigning high priest. For ours is a world in which not only development is at work, but degeneration also. The Jewish religion, in its purer, fairer forms, had fallen from the heights and been picked up by the defiled hands of Annas, Caiaphas, and their unholy conspirators. Surely this is one of the horrible facts of history: Sometimes the holiest is seized upon by the most hellish, which keeps a temporary upper hand. Then do men look up and behold heavens of iron; look out and behold horizons of gloom; look down and behold soundless seas of sorrow.

The Realism and Idealism of Life

As a flashlight turned upon those two spots of humanized darkness, Annas and Caiaphas, consider the law governing witnesses in the Sanhedrin. In the first place, the witness for the defense was first examined; in the second place, a corroborating witness was required before the testimony of the first witness became legal. Essentially, it was a wise law; its aim was to guarantee justice to all appearing before that august tribunal. But what have we in the case of Jesus? This: *"Now the chief priests and the whole council sought false witnesses against Jesus, that they might put Him to death."* Even religion —the holiest, cleanest, deepest power God implants in the human soul—forsook Jesus, and took refuge in hearts of hatred and minds of malice.

We sometimes compare the last hours of Socrates with those of Christ. The immortal Greek surely behaved himself with heroism and nobility. The grandeur of Socrates reveals, in contrast, the meanness of his judges. But the difference, my friends, in the trial of Socrates and the trial of Christ is this: It is just the immeasurable difference between the philosopher and the Saviour. If you fail to see it, no argument of mine will convince you. It is not a matter that can be decided by argument. Ultimately, it is the reaction of our own souls to that which is secondary and that which is supreme.

When a man says that Socrates and Christ belong in the same category, he is properly judging neither, but pronouncing judgment upon himself. And self-judgment, next to the judgment of the wise, good God, is the most searching judgment the moral universe can show. Forsaken by the religion of his own nation, I can easily imagine Socrates, in a universe like this, carrying his case to the Supreme Court of the Christ. Likewise forsaken by the religion of His own nation, by no stretch of the imagination could I picture Jesus, in a universe such as ours, carrying His wrongs to a tribunal occupied by Socrates. "For neither doth the Father judge any man," says Jesus, "but He hath given all judgment unto the Son; that all may honor the Son even as they honor the Father. He that honoreth not the Son honoreth not the Father that sent Him." Imagine Socrates speaking these words! He would have brought upon himself centuries of philosophic laughter. But Jesus speaks them, and the Soul of the Universe, as well as Christianized human consciousness, utters its grand Amen! Verily, religion was horribly unjust to itself when it forsook Jesus that night two thousand years ago.

Jesus was forsaken by Law. "And the same day Pilate and Herod were made friends together: for before they were at enmity between themselves."

The Realism and Idealism of Life

Did evil ever lift its sinister face and wear a more wicked smile than upon that day when Pilate and Herod, separated by fires of hatred, are drawn together in their mutual antagonism to Christ? Yet, strange as it is, it is by no means uncommon in life. Let two bad men, avowed enemies, be confronted by one good man, and the two bad men, by a kind of moral gravitation, will be pulled toward each other rather than toward the man in whom goodness lives. So Pilate and Herod, the right and left arms of what we call law and order, found in Jesus, the incarnation of justice and truth, a common ground upon which they might stand and reunite the broken ties of a wicked friendship. For one brief moment Pilate, alone with Jesus—"always with that high look of Godlike calm"—and wrought upon by His nameless power, seems to see a tiny flame of goodness flaring up amid the burned-out cinders of his ruined soul. Guided by that feeble, flickering light, he came out and said to the Jews: "I find no crime in Him." And yet Pilate scourged Him, allowed his soldiers to crown Him with thorns, mock Him, and smite Him. Likewise, Herod and his soldiers mocked Him, dressed Him in gorgeous robes of derision, and shunted Him about as if He were a common criminal.

Yet, forsaken by Friendship and Religion and Law, does not Jesus reach the acme of forsakenness as revealed in His question on the Cross: "My God, my God, why hast thou forsaken me?" In a swiftly darkening world order He seems to be finally enclosed by impenetrable darkness. Has the God whose will it was His delight always to do—has He, too, forsaken Him? Has the Father whose deeds of mercy He had joyfully performed—has He given up His Son to the unmerciful? It is one of the darkest, most mysterious moments in the whole history of mind. Perhaps, after all, it is not unthinkable that the disciples should forsake Him. The spirit is willing, but the flesh is weak. It is horrible, but not impossible, for religion to become so perverted as to lose its inherent majesty. And law, in the course of this world, often loses its way, falling among the enemies of order and justice and truth. But here, at last, is the question that crushes the Son of Man: "My God, my God, why hast thou forsaken me?"

Now, what I want to know is this: Will God answer the question? Verily, He will! He is the only Person Who can answer it. And His answer must be written in deeds so wonderful that all history, all thought, all art, all music, all eloquence, all faith, all hope, all love shall spend their being in trying to tell how God answers the question of His beloved Son upon the Cross. Meantime, we shall have to journey from the Cross to the Garden; we shall have to go in behind the stifling realism of life and behold life's imperishable idealism.

II

Consider, therefore, the idealism of life as it utters itself in our second text: "Go unto my brethren and say to them, I ascend unto my Father and your Father, and my God and your God." These are the words of the Master to Mary as she stood weeping and worshipful at the entrance of the empty tomb. And what words of life are these, deep with deathless beauty, alive with the wonder and wisdom of Godhood! "O woman, with the lily heart and the Easter hope, go tell My brethren that I ascend. I have descended into the uttermost depths. I have found desolate wastes where Friends forsake and Religion denies and Law perverts. But I have endured them all; I have wrung from death the last bitter drop within its poisoned being; I have gone with the outgoing tides to the uttermost deeps of doom. But now the tides have turned. Deep and swift and strong they are bearing Me back to the Eternal Hills of Home, whence I came here to share the lot of immortal seamen, wrecked upon the coasts of time. Yea, Mary, weep not. Go to My brethren

285

—the brethren who forsook Me and fled—go to them and say, My God, Who seemed to have forsaken Me, hath not suffered His Holy One to see corruption, but hath raised Me from the dead and led captivity captive."

Oh, yes, there is plenty of realism in life. But there is *more*—there is deathless and undefeatable idealism. Do you say that His friends forsook Jesus? Well, but consider this: Those disciples, at that particular period of their development, did not spell out the full significance of friendship. Look at them later, after they have journeyed to the world's end under the budding skies of that Friendship Divine! You will find nothing grander in history than the way those first men and women responded to the pull of Christ from within the worlds out of sight. Bow your heads in shame at the denying, swearing Peter, remembering that we, too, have presented just as abject spectacles of failure. But, oh! do not forget that other Peter—the Peter of the unpublished Easter morning talk with his Lord; the Peter of Pentecost; the Peter of the cross, crucified head downward; the Peter of the Christian centuries who, just because of his mixture of weakness and strength, has brought hope to the struggling millions in their fight to win their souls for God and truth. See, also, that young Pharisee, persecuting

286

to the death those who had found the Way. Behold him red-handed, ranging like a wild beast his ways of destruction. Employ any figure of speech to set forth the desperation of Saul of Tarsus, and you will hardly equal the persecutor himself. But lo! that blood-thirsty Saul becomes the life-giving, kingdom-building Paul. As an exhibition of sheer will-power, measured by what he did in influencing cities, continents, and civilizations, I can think of no being in the known universe capable of mastering Saul of Tarsus except the Christ of God. But He did it—did it grandly, did it in such wise that the splendor of that noonday sun pales before the transfiguring light with which the glorified Christ enveloped the Apostle to the Gentiles.

We do wrong in thinking only of our imperfect and ungrown friendships. Friendship that could be entirely exploited in the fields of time would not wear well in the spheres of eternity. After all, we are scarcely beyond the embryonic stage in these high matters. These October days have spread a magic across the land. It steals not alone into the dreamful faces of humans, but it seems to stir our little friends, the caterpillars, to unwonted activity. They are in the grass, in the roadways, even upon the doorsteps. Out there on Michigan Avenue, this morning as I was going north, I met one of these prophet-creatures coming south. Pausing, I said: "Good morning, Mr. Caterpillar. Whither bound?" He was so absorbed in the business of creeping that he scarcely deigned to answer me. But as he kept creeping—creeping—creeping, he looked back and said: "Why, Man, I'm on my way to get my wings. Don't bother me." I laughed and at once took my seat among the scornful. "Your wings?" I rejoined. "What on earth have you to do with wings?" "What have I to do with wings?" he answered, creeping—creeping—creeping along. "Why, I have wings inside of me this very moment. I'm going to unpack them one of these days. Come around next June and I will show you my wings instead of this worm." And are we not all embryonic humans? We spend our years in the valley between dust and divinity. Two natures are ever struggling within us. "The man of prehistoric times lives on, unchanged, in our Unconscious," says Freud. But never mind! The mountain of divinity shall absorb the mountain of dust, the two struggling natures within shall be finally harmonized, the man of prehistoric times shall be changed into the man of times eternal. For God will perfect that which concerneth us. And more than earth concerns us, more than death and the grave. Smitten with a sick man's fancy, Coleridge wrote Charles Lamb asking forgiveness for some fancied wrong. Lamb replied in the following post-script, which deserves to be immortal: "If you ever thought an offense, much more wrote it, against me, it must have been in the times of Noah, and the great waters have swept it away. Mary is crying for mere love of your letter." Well, if human friendship can dress itself in such lovely hues, think it not strange that the Divine Friendship shall go on working its miracles of grace—now setting the wayward feet of a Peter upon solid rock, now turning the discordant will of a Saul into the undying love of the Paul of Corinthians Thirteen. Thirteen may be an unlucky number; but I like to remember that one of the transcendent chapters in all literature bears the name Thirteen and has also Thirteen incomparable verses.

Did you say that Religion forsook the Master? I beg your pardon! That was just a slip of the tongue, and you must instantly apologize. It was only make-believe and petrified hypocrisy, which had become temporarily housed in the Sanhedrin, that mistreated the Master. Pure religion and undefiled forsake Him? Why, you might as well talk of flowers forsaking their stems, of rains forsaking the clouds, of sunbeams forsaking the sun. But even in that horrible night of realism, consider how the truth asserts itself. Go back to the Cross again. Nature seems to be putting on black, as if to hide her face from the baseness of men. While priests mock and soldiers gamble and mobs sway to and fro, one of those two thieves breaks through walls of hate and ventures into gardens of faith. "Jesus," he cried, as the worlds reeled around and within him, "remember me when thou comest in thy kingdom." Ponder this: When His own friends had temporarily fallen away, true Religion steps forth from the soul of a criminal, beholds the majesty of our dying Lord, and prays for a place in His undying Kingdom. Over against the wickedness of high priest and king and governor, I like to set the faith of the repentant thief. A grain of true faith in Jesus Christ will outweigh mountains of iniquity. Paint your realism "black as the pit, from pole to pole," but, remember, it is not the whole, it is not even on speaking terms with the permanent and true. For while sin runs amuck in high places and truth is ignored in low, God will find Him room even in the most unexpected house of human nature and gloriously dwell therein.

Think, too, of Mary Magdalene. You say that Religion was struck a hard blow by Annas and Caiaphas. I tell you the world-deep devotion of Mary Magdalene is bright enough to illumine their darkness. Every Gospel tells about Mary. There are some facts connected with the Life of Lives reported by one Evangelist and omitted by others. But Mary—sin-wounded, Christ-forgiven Mary— walks through all the Gospels of the Easter morning like some royally crowned queen come down from the High Hills of God. When the love of God in Christ laid hold of Mary, it found a human being who could stand by the Cross, weep through the night as her woman's hands prepared the spices of love, beat the sun up in the morning, and run over the hills of Bethany to catch the first human glimpse of the Risen One! Has not Mary become a kind of voice for all struggling, aspiring, climbing, falling souls the world around? Thus a modern poet has, through Mary, uttered a truth that all of us should heed:

> O Magdalene, I, too, have known the longing
>   To kneel and wash with tears the Saviour's feet;
> To dry them with my tresses and anoint them
>   With blessed myrrh and ointment, rare and sweet.
>
> But I have not the courage that God gave you;
>   I could not bear the wise men's piercing eyes.
> Before a sneering glance my heart would falter;
>   I would deny their scorn with shameful lies.
>
> And still I go to church each Sunday morning
>   And think upon our dear Lord crucified.
> I yearn to kneel before His feet for comfort
>   And kiss His hands and touch His wounded side.

291

Frederick F. Shannon

If I should cry, my burning tears would shame me,
    And those who sit in every near-by row
Would turn their scornful glances on my sorrow;
    I could not bear to have the whole world know.

And so I sit a hypocrite, contented
    To know that only God can see my soul.
O Magdalene, plead well for me in Heaven,
    That Christ may cleanse my heart and make me whole.

But did not Law forsake Him? Did not the rules of civilized society, as reflected by Rome and Jerusalem, break down under the strain of injustice and yield up the Christ to wild, insane forces of disorder? In answer to these questions, we should do some straight, hard thinking. In the first place, the sense of law and order did not *originate* with Memphis, Babylon, Athens, Rome, or Jerusalem. The sense of order is primarily in the heart and mind of God. In behind protoplasm, the physical basis of life, law and order are in perfect operation. They are in the stellar worlds and in the atomic galaxies, in the illimitably great and the infinitely small. Now, is the idea of physical order more deeply ingrained in the warp and woof things than the idea of moral order? In other words, is the physical anterior to and superior to the spiritual? It is utterly unthinkable! Law and order, let me repeat, did not begin with the world, nor can it end with the world.

The Realism and Idealism of Life

In the history of human thought, few men have done more to give this idea worthy expression than Richard Hooker. He, too, belongs to that marvelous sixteenth century. He belongs with your Shakespeare and Bacon and Milton and Spenser and Raleigh. One of the amplest souls that ever lived— great in his learning, great in his piety, great in his humanness—Hooker combines the best of the ancients and the moderns. Dying at the age of forty-seven, when the Fundamentalists of his time were misinterpreting the very religion they professed, Hooker asked: "May we cause our faith without Reason to appear reasonable in the eyes of men?" And then, of this original, uncreated law which holds the worlds together, he says, in one of the noblest passages in all literature: "Wherefore, that here we may briefly end: of law there can be no less acknowledged, than that her seat is the bosom of God, her voice the harmony of the world: all things in Heaven and earth do her homage, the very least as feeling her care, and the greatest as not exempted from her power; both angels and men and creatures of what condition soever, though each in different sort and manner, yet all with uniform consent, admiring her as the mother of their peace and their joy." More than three hundred years ago what did the great Hooker say but this: The idea of law did not begin with this world, and, therefore, it cannot end with this world.

In the second place, how can law ultimately forsake its Creator? Those to whom the administration of the organized laws of society is entrusted may prove unequal to their obligations and privileges. But their reign, in the long view, is temporary, brief, soon gone. But He—the Divine Original of Law—abides forever, and cannot be forsaken by that which is the breath of His own being and Godhead. Therefore, what an answer does Jesus give to Pilate! Nettled by the Master's speechful silence, Pilate asked: "Knowest thou not that I have power to release thee, and have power to crucify thee?" Calmly and with Godlike restraint the Master replied: "Thou couldest have no power against me, except it were given thee from above." In short, Cæsar, Pilate, Herod, Annas, and Caiaphas—all alike were even then within the grip of that very Power "from above"—the law of God, of Right, of Truth—which they were wickedly perverting and against which they were vainly contending.

Forsaken by Law? Oh, no! Our Lord could not be forsaken by that which owes its being to Him. Men may violate Christ's law and destroy themselves. But that law is indestructible. Indeed, one of the most solemn facts of our era for the whole wide world is this: By ignoring Christ's law for individuals and nations, mankind may pull down the house of civilization upon itself. We emphasize the beauty of doing that which is right; we must also emphasize the horror of doing that which is wrong. We say: "What a fine thing it would be if all nations could be so organized as to outlaw war." Ah, but we must also say: "All nations *must* be so organized, or else war shall utterly destroy the nations." And the genius of such an organization must be filled with the Spirit of Christ; otherwise it must fall under its own load of mechanical ineffectiveness. But whatever men and nations do, or refuse to do, set this down as inviolable truth: Law cannot forsake the Christ of God any more than light can forsake the sun from which it streams. He—and He alone—

> He shall lay on souls the power of Peace,
>   And send on kingdoms torn the sense of Home,
> More than the fire of Joy that burned on Greece,
>   More than the light of Law that rose on Rome.

Finally, was He not forsaken of God? Did He not himself cry from His Hill of Pain: "My God, my God, why hast thou forsaken me?" Here, indeed, would we stand in awe upon the verse of mysterious realms. The full meaning of these words cannot be disclosed. Beyond the powers of thought did the anguish of our Lord's vicarious passion fling him forth into the dreadful wastes of No Man's Land of Sin and Death. Yet are we absolutely sure that in the darkest moment in the experience of the moral universe, He was not forsaken of God. The God Whose Eternal Son He is; the God from Whose bosom He came; the God Whose wisdom He spake; the God Whose works He wrought—surely God was well-pleased with such a humanized transcript of His own inexhaustible self-giving in that hour when both the outer and inner suns seemingly refused their light to the Saviour of the world. Hunting the universe through and waiting the cycles long, God had at last found One Who, in the spheres of humanity, could perfectly experience and interpret His love to a lost world. Forsaken of God? Why, God raised Him from the dead and gave unto Him the Name that is above every name, whether in hell or earth or sky.

So, it seems to me, does our holy religion introduce us to the realism of life. But it does not stop there —it goes straight through the dark and terrible realism into the Heart of Infinite Love wherein our white and conquering idealism everlastingly abides. Penetrating below all deeps of darkness, it ranges beyond all heights of light and love. Upon our own Hills of Agony, we, too, sometimes cry: "Why hast

Thou forsaken Me?" But hard by the Darkening Hill is a Garden all golden with the Light of the Resurrection Morning. Standing by the entrance of life's empty tombs, we may still hear One say: "Go unto my brethren and say unto them, I ascend unto my Father and your Father, and my God and your God." Oh, is it not the history of One Man standing against the universe, only to find the universe swinging at last over to His side, proclaiming Him King of kings and Lord of lords!

> But now Thou art in the Shadowless Land,
>   Behind the light of the setting Sun;
> And the worst is forgotten which Evil planned,
>   And the best which Love's glory could win is won.

THE NATURE OF RELIGION

Preacher, pastor, scholar, bookman, poet, Dr. Hough is one of the most gifted and influential men in the American pulpit, his prodigious studentship only equaled by his personal and intellectual charm. Born in Ohio in 1877, educated at Union College, Drew Seminary, and New York University, after various pastorates in New Jersey, Long Island, Brooklyn and Baltimore, he became professor of Historical Theology in Garrett Biblical Institute, Evanston; and finally president of Northwestern University in 1919. He is now minister of Central Methodist Church in Detroit, where he holds a unique position of influence in a brilliant city. To name the books written by Dr. Hough, from *Athanasius, Hero* to *Synthetic Christianity* or *The Imperial Voice*—the last perhaps his best volume of sermons—would be to turn this note into a catalogue of sermons, essays, stories, poems, lectures on theological and philosophical topics, with an appendix devoted to editorials, dialogues, and patriotic addresses. He is as well and widely known in England as in America, made so, first, by his mission as lecturer on the moral and spiritual aims of the war on the Lindgren foundation of Northwestern University in 1918, and as holiday preacher at the City Temple the same year. He is a most attractive university preacher, as witness the following sermon, as much for his mastery of a limpid, vivid, musical style—delicate without being dainty, flexible and forthright, rich in color cadence—as for his clear insight and wise guidance in those pathways by which groping man finds his way to the Eternal amid the fogs and illusions of time.

THE NATURE OF RELIGION

LYNN HAROLD HOUGH, TH.D., LITT.D.

CENTRAL METHODIST CHURCH, DETROIT

"God—hath—spoken to us in his Son." Hebrews 1: 1, 2.

There is a suggestive passage in the Odyssey describing the meeting of Hermes and the goddess Calypso when Zeus has sent the messenger of the gods to require the release of Odysseus:

> But Calypso, goddess bright,
> Failed not to know him, seeing him face to face;
> For never do the Gods' immortal race
> Fail to know one another when they meet,
> How far soe'er apart their dwelling place.

That instant recognition of the divine by the divine is the very heart of religion. It is an immediate and authentic consciousness of a world of realities and values existing in its own right.

In a period full of energetic activity and moved by all the challenge of the gospel of action it is very easy for us to confuse religion with the products which flow from it. So religion becomes a program of activity, a method of human living, a social syn-

301

thesis. So it becomes the mind in action for productive thinking, the heart in action interpreting all feeling and beauty, the will in action dominating the relations of men. It becomes the moral and spiritual and esthetic conscience of men. All this is splendidly wholesome when it is seen as the fruit of religion rather than its seed, the harvest of religion rather than its root. But all of this is likely to become cold and barren at last unless we keep in touch with religion in its more fundamental relations, at its creative source.

The difference is very well illustrated by two significant little books recently published. One is *When Evolution and Religion Meet,* by Professor John M. Coulter and Professor Merle C. Coulter. The other is *A Living Universe,* by Principal L. P. Jacks of Manchester College, Oxford. The volume *When Evolution and Religion Meet* is a most useful introduction to various types of evolutionary theory. It is written with a fine sympathy with the ideals of Jesus. It is one of those pieces of honest and careful work for which we all ought to be grateful. But never once does it sound the fundamental note of religion. Science and the principles of Jesus meet in a noble fashion in this book. But evolution and religion do not meet because religion does not appear.

The Nature of Religion

On the other hand Principal Jacks brings you into the most definite contact with the very genius of religion. Of course he is very candid and open-minded in respect of all the great contributions of science. But to him biology itself speaks the language of religion. Science itself glows with the wonder of a religious experience. And in *A Living Universe* science and religion do meet. You close the book with quickened heart beat. Floods of inspiration are released and move all through your personality. Science glows with the glory of religion and religion is seen as the consummation of science. What was prose in the work of the Professors Coulter is creative poetry with Principal Jacks. What was information in their useful volume is inspiration in his seminal lectures.

Altogether it may seem wise for us this morning to spend a little while thinking of the nature of religion. There is nothing foreign to it. But some things are basal in it. And it will clarify our thinking and enrich our living if we can get down to some of these basal matters.

I

Religion is a personal discovery. It is not something we can hand on to others. It is something we

303

meet in the depths of our own experience. In a sense this is of course true of all the great matters. Even in conversation you cannot plant a thought in another man's mind. You can only give him an opportunity with a flash of interested discovery to find that thought for himself. It is easy to over-emphasize social solidarity in the fundamental matters of life. And religion especially is never the creative experience to which the word really belongs when it is second hand. When it is authentic it comes with the sudden glory of a personal discovery. And it takes strange forms. Lucretius' *De Rerum Natura* may seem a fundamental attack on religion. But that stately order to which the Latin poet appeals from the wild anarchy of the gods of Olympus is itself a reality warm with all the beautiful wonder of religion to the followers of Epicurus. *Thus Spake Zarathustra* may seem the most deadly sort of attack on religion. But the apotheosis of the assertive will as over against the submissive will had all the glow of a religious experience to Nietzsche. To be sure there was not enough substance to the discovery of Lucretius to feed the spirit of humanity. And the discovery of Nietzsche left one-sided and alone was the sort of thing which breaks down human life. But each in his own way and in his own degree had contact with a truth which glowed brightly and kindled all the devotion of religion. There is a difference between a religion and an adequate religion. But religion itself covers a wide area.

To keep the note of discovery is the great battle of the historic religions. There are forces at work in all of them which tend to reduce the whole structure to commonplaceness and dullness and convention. The battle between the prophets and the priests is the perpetual conflict between the discoverers and those who have no fresh contact with reality.

This discovery must be made in the terms of the contemporary life and vernacular if it is to have the widest influences and power. In this sense it is rather unfortunate that we think of the canon of the Old and New Testaments as closed. For a closed form of experience is all too likely to mean for many men a literary prison beyond whose walls they dare not go. It was fortunate for the Jewish exiles that Ezekiel could use thought-forms growing out of life in Babylonia. It was fortunate for early Christians that Paul could use thought-forms growing out of the Roman Empire's vast and unified life. We need to claim the same sort of liberty to-day.

For many a man the happiest approach to religion is through the whole biological process. Indeed we may go further and say that the whole cosmological process is a great introduction to religion. Beginning with the first thrust of life from the water upon the land, on to the highest forms of life, beginning with the mutual aid seen all through the biological process, on to the greatness of motherhood which is self-sacrifice alive; beginning with the first movement of mind among the creatures of this world on to the fulness of understanding of its greatest thinkers; beginning with the first outreach of man for God on to the perfect consciousness of fellowship with God which lived in Jesus; we may see the biological process itself as the expression of God at work in the world. As a notable contemporary teacher of science has said, we see "Jesus Christ to be the crown of the evolutionary process." And as the vision of the whole forward moving process with God moving through and in it for his own high aims possesses a man's soul he begins to feel that the whole biological process is back of him and with him pushing him forward in every moral and spiritual battle. It is the moment of discovery when the facts science brings to light take on this moral and spiritual meaning that religion is born as a personal experience. Science itself becomes the mother of a commanding and creative mysticism. This is not the only approach to a personal experience of religion. But it is a very happy and nobly fruitful approach in our time.

The Nature of Religion

The second characteristic of religion which should command our attention is this. It is a perpetual personal adventure. Donald Hankey put this insight into a striking phrase: "Religion is betting your life that there is a God." There is always an element of noble risk. And when we stop to think of it, only by taking risks in the name of what ought to be, can character possibly grow. If you could reduce beauty to a mathematical formula the soul of the love of beauty as a personal experience would vanish. If you could reduce right and wrong to a demonstrated process of reasoning the wonder of the moral life would disappear. If you could reduce religion to absolute certainty religious experience would cease to be a creative and fruitful experience. It is just because all these things have an aspect of glorious adventure that they call for that courage and that dauntless enthusiasm which lie at the root of the greatest sort of character. The heroes of religion belong to the same line as the great discoverers and the great pioneers. They go forth in the name of a dauntless ideal and an expectant faith. They are all the while believing in unknown lands beyond the tempestuous seas. And they are all the while sailing forth to make these lands their own.

Lynn Harold Hough, Th.D., Litt.D.

When religion becomes organized and when its beliefs become codified there is always the tendency to forget this element of gay and heroic adventure. But personal Christian experience always keeps alive what the ecclesiastical system and the authoritative dogma would let die. For the personal experience of religion is always an act of dauntless faith. Herein is the preservation of the virility of religion, and herein is its perpetual appeal to the strong men who build empires and to the audacious spirits whom "only the farthest beacons beckon." There is a notable place for organization. And there is a profound significance in dogma. But the life of these must perpetually be renewed by the experience of religion as a personal adventure.

All of this is strikingly clear in the experience of Jesus with his disciples. There is a perpetual air of freshness and vitality about the whole enterprise. When Jesus says, "Follow me," he is calling men to the most heroic sort of adventure. There is the thrill of high romance. There is the poetry of the spirit which eagerly takes great risks. There is a sense of springtime and beautiful verdure. There is the bloom and fragrance of exquisite flowers. There is the promise of abundant harvest. There is life glowing and triumphant everywhere.

When you follow the amazing journeys of the
308

The Nature of Religion

Apostle Paul you are in the presence of the spirit of dauntless adventure. You feel the very pulse beats of an heroic faith. Paul would have understood the quality of Tennyson's *Ulysses*.

> 'Tis not too late to seek a newer world;
> Push off, and sitting well in order smite
> The sounding furrows; for my purpose holds
> To sail beyond the sunset, and the baths
> Of all the western stars, until I die.
> It may be that the gulfs will wash us down;
> It may be we shall touch the Happy Isles;
> And see the great Achilles whom we knew.
> Tho' much is taken, much abides, and tho'
> We are not now that strength which in old days
> Moved earth and heaven; that which we are, we are,
> One equal temper of heroic hearts,
> Made weak by time and fate but strong in will
> To strive, to seek, to find, and not to yield.

The men and women who have pursued the paths of Christian experience with the most exhaustless eagerness give us constantly the high sense of personal adventure. The fourteenth century Bedford tinker put this insight into immortal English in *Pilgrim's Progress*. Whenever Christianity is truly alive it is a vital flame in the soul of the Christian. And that flame lights the way on an endless adventure of the spirit.

Lynn Harold Hough, Th.D., Litt.D.

III

Religion is an experience of certainty. It is the conscious meeting of time and eternity. It is the far-flying bird coming at last to its nest. It is humanity finding its home in the heart of God. But the very nature of this certainty is that it comes after the adventure and not before it. Indeed it comes at the very moment when all the risks are taken and the whole personality is put into the adventure whatever it costs. The hour of illuminated certainty is the hour of unhesitating daring. To use the great word of Jesus "when we will to do we know." Certainty as a moral and spiritual experience of the personal life is not a static or rigid thing. It is a rich and growing experience of satisfaction. It is the assurance of the bird on the wing. It is the certainty which comes in the experience of flight.

Dr. Barbour's biography of that great Scottish preacher, Alexander Whyte, who preached to the conscience of the English-speaking world as did no other man of his time, gives the reader the sense of a kind of high and aroused conviction of the reality of moral and spiritual things. And the discerning reader cannot fail to see that this abounding confidence was the ever-renewed assurance of a man who all his life was making new adventures of going forth in utter dependence upon the living God. Christian certainty is the freest and most creative thing in all the world.

IV

The Christian religion is fellowship with a Christ-like God. The consummation of religion is the personal appropriation of the insight that the living God is like Jesus Christ. That Jesus expressed in time what God is in Eternity is the central matter in the Christian faith. That as we look into the face of Christ we look into the face of God is the ultimate matter of Christian experience.

The moral experience of Jesus in relation to goodness and evil, love and hate, brotherhood and selfishness, is the expression of the very character of God within the area of human life. And the cross with its exhaustless passion for goodness and its exhaustless love for men and women caught in the meshes of evil, that rescuing splendor of sacrificial love, is the glowing center of the Christian religion. To see God through the eye which Jesus gives us is to make the great moral and spiritual discovery. To enter into fellowship with him is the supreme adventure of daring faith. To live in the light of that adventure is to find certainty as faith becomes action. To seek above all things in the individual life and in

311

all social and corporate relations the will of the God whose face we see in the face of Christ is to become a vital part of the Kingdom of God in the world. Religion begins in discovery and adventure. It ends in Christlike character. It begins as an experience of the individual. It comes to its consummation in a transformed society. Dante's rose of love and fire is the symbol of the final bloom of religion in time and in eternity.

THE TRUE PROTESTANTISM

Dr. Merrill is a New Jersey man, born at Orange in 1867, educated at Rutgers College and Union Theological Seminary, and was ordained to the Presbyterian ministry in 1890. After important pastorates in Trinity Church, Philadelphia, and the Sixth Church of Chicago, he came to the Brick Church in New York, where he has had a distinguished ministry both as preacher and Christian leader. With the passion of a prophet he unites a practical acumen and poise of judgment—something more than astuteness—which makes him sagacious and inspiring in counsel. As president of the Board of the Church Peace Union, he is a leader equally in the movements toward Christian unity and international comity, whereof we read in *The Common Creed Christians* and *Christian Internationalism*. This sermon is characteristic of his qualities, alike in its temper and its teaching, and is a notable plea in behalf of a positive, constructive Protestantism, bringing the old values of faith to the service of the new vision of the world and its need: a comprehensive, forward-looking Church, uniting different points of view in one sovereign loyalty, never better expounded than in his Yale lectures on the liberty of the pulpit.

THE TRUE PROTESTANTISM

WILLIAM P. MERRILL, D.D.

THE BRICK CHURCH, NEW YORK

"The just shall live by faith." Romans 1: 17.

Three hundred years ago, at about this time in the year, a little company of some thirty families, Walloons by race, Protestants in religion, sailed into the mouth of the Hudson River and settled, a few here on Manhattan, more where Albany now stands. They came, as the Pilgrims had come to Plymouth four years before, that they might escape from persecution and be free to worship God according to their own best light. Like the Pilgrims, they had been for years guests in the hospitable land of Holland, and had gained much in their sojourn there. Much honor has been paid to the Dutch settlers of New Amsterdam, and more to the Puritan settlers of New England. We do well to remember these French men and women who contributed not a little to those religious and moral forces which have made our country great and strong. Their blood is in our veins, and their spirit is in our souls. It is quite impossible to estimate the debt owed by the free

315

modern world to those Huguenot exiles, who were driven from France in large numbers by the cruelty and folly of bigoted rulers. Their descendants came with the English settlers to New England and with the Dutch to New Netherlands. We are glad to honor their memory in this service.

It would be of doubtful value to use the sermon time in a historical statement about this little company. When we have said that they were French Protestants, exiled for fidelity to their religion to Holland, and coming to these shores for further freedom and opportunity, we have said all that need be said. It will honor these sturdy pioneers far more, and meet far better the needs of our own time, if we think about that Protestant spirit which was so dear to them, and how it may be effective in our own day—that Protestantism for which they were cheerfully ready to "suffer the loss of all things." The best use we can make of an honored past is to carry it forward into an honorable future.

Let us then, in grateful appreciation of these men of three centuries ago, and of their heroic stand for the truth of God as they saw and felt it, think of the present demand and need for a truly Protestant faith and spirit.

The times demand a revival of true Protestantism. That is one of the great and vital needs of the present

316

The True Protestantism

world-situation. That does not mean that we need an anti-Catholic spirit or movement. It is unfortunate that to some the word "Protestant" means above all a spirit and movement antagonistic to the Roman Catholic Church, and to the Catholic idea or tendency in certain sections of Protestantism. No doubt we do need ever to be quietly on guard against the encroachments of *priestliness*. There is something in autocracy which makes freemen watchful if they are wise. "Eternal vigilance is the price of liberty." Dean Hodges well said, "Religion in every age needs both the prophet and the priest. But the prophet can be trusted; the priest needs to be watched."

But a Protestantism, which is in the main an anti-Romanism, is a pitiful thing. To be "anti" anything is a poor sort of business. There are altogether too many people in the world to-day satisfied to hold a critical position, to be *opposed* to something, or to everything. The revival of Protestantism which is needed is not an increase of such a critical and negative attitude. To stand up for Protestantism is not at all synonymous with standing against Romanism.

Indeed we have grossly misused and misread the very word "Protestant." Many people have confessed a dislike for the name on the ground that they do not want to be labeled as eternally entering protest, forever objecting to something or somebody.

William P. Merrill, D.D.

But a very little thought and study shows that that is a complete misunderstanding of a great and honorable word. Those of us who retain even a fragment of our knowledge of Latin know that that first syllable, "pro" means not "against," but "for"; and that the root "test" means "bearing witness." Look in a good lexicon, and you find that the idea of objecting to something, the notion of a critical or antagonistic attitude is a secondary or remote meaning of the word "protest." The primary meaning is to "make a solemn affirmation," "to bear witness to a truth or belief one holds." It is unfortunate that the word "protest" has come to be associated with critical or pugnacious acts, has acquired an implication of being in the opposition, and is even associated with bad checks. We need to get back to the original and real meaning. The *Protestant* is one who is ready to bear testimony on behalf of something real and vital. He is a witness, a martyr in the original sense of that great word.

We need also to make clear the fact that, when we call for a re-assertion of the Protestant faith and spirit, we are not urging a more strict adherence to the traditions and definitions of the Protestantism of the sixteenth and seventeenth centuries.

The leaders of the Reformation formulated their theological convictions in great creeds and treatises.

318

The True Protestantism

These are noble documents; in the main they express the true Protestant convictions for our day as for the day in which and for which they were prepared. But that which we so greatly need is not a rigid adherence to these doctrinal statements. It is always wrong to exalt form above spirit: it is more than wrong, it is treason, for Protestants to do that. John Robinson, leader of the English Puritan exiles in Holland, called by one of his most bitter enemies "the most learned, polished, and modest spirit that ever separated from the Church of England," told the little band of Pilgrims in his farewell address at Delftshaven that one serious trouble in the Protestant churches was the tendency of both Calvinists and Lutherans to "stick where Calvin and Luther left them." Both Calvin and Luther, he declared, were great and shining lights in their day; but God had new truth for the new day, which should be seized and followed as eagerly as Calvin and Luther followed the truth they saw. The essence of Protestantism is in a spirit, not in creeds or forms It is that Protestant spirit which needs revival, re-assertion, to-day as the essential attitude of free Christian souls.

What are the chief elements of this true Protestant spirit and attitude?

Its fundamental position is the right of the individual soul to find God for himself. No man or church can say to the free human spirit, "You must find God in this way, or you cannot find Him at all." God is not bound up in any sacraments, or in any writings, nor is He closeted in any church buildings or holy places. His ministers, whether they be called priests or presbyters (and John Milton's keen thrust still has point to it, that "presbyter is only priest writ large") are here to be useful to men, but not to rule over their souls; to be servants, not lords. The leaders of the Reformation insisted strongly on "the universal priesthood of believers." Every man is meant to find God, to know God, to live with God, for himself, without the dictation of any ecclesiastical authority. The moment any priest, or any ecclesiastical body whatever, attempts to say just what the individual believer shall believe, or how he shall pray, or what he shall do, it is time for the true Protestant to stand up and protest, not only bearing witness against spiritual tyranny, but bearing his testimony for spiritual freedom and the right of the individual soul to find God for itself, and to live in the light that comes from Him.

But Protestantism is not unregulated individualism. The true Protestant is not a spiritual anarchist. The Reformers clearly discerned a second fundamental principle, to be combined and balanced with the right of the individual soul and conscience—the principle of the supreme authority of the Bible in matters of faith and conduct. They recognized the fact that we are not only individuals, but social beings, realizing our best selves only in relation with other men and with God. Therefore they rightly saw that there must be an agreement on some common standard. With great daring they cast aside the authority of pope and council, of creed and custom and tradition, and affirmed that the word of God, which we call the Bible, is the *"only* infallible rule of faith and conduct."

The wisest among them were careful to guard well this declaration of the supreme authority of the Scriptures, that it might not become simply another rigid external authority over the free souls of men. Carefully they stated that its authority extends not to all matters, not to history, or science, or philosophy, but "what we are to believe concerning God, and what duty God requires of man." Strenuously they insisted that the word of God is not to become a new law, binding the soul. Emphatically they declared that it is not to be held subject to any one credal interpretation, that it is superior to all creeds and forms and counsels of men. It is inspiring to read the Westminster Confession of Faith, and find that strong massive statement of doctrine so elastic

321

William P. Merrill, D.D.

and vital in its idea of the Bible, always insisting that our faith in its authority comes, not from any man or church, or from any external proofs, but from the spirit of God witnessing in our hearts as we read; that the plain man is to go freely to the Bible for his guidance; that the scholar is to go freely to the original sources of the Bible and study them with open mind; that the supreme Judge is always the Holy Spirit speaking in the Scriptures. In every possible way true Protestants have always guarded, as equally precious, essential each to the other, neither one ever to be surrendered to the other, the divine authority of the Bible, and the right of private judgment on truth and duty. The glory of the true Protestant spirit and attitude is this well-balanced faith in the Bible and in the conscience and soul of the believer. It believes heartily in both. It is not afraid to leave them alone together. It puts the Bible—unaccompanied by any authoritative interpretation, this rich, varied, glorious, wild-flower-garden of a book, into the hands of every believer, and says to him, "Here is your guide; you can trust its guidance better than you can trust any other. Use your intellect honestly upon it; face what it says; fit it to your actual life; practise what you find in it; and you shall be guided without fail as to your faith and conduct."

The True Protestantism

These are the two great foundations of the Protestant position, the supreme right of the individual to find God for himself, and the supreme authority of the Bible as God's word to the soul.

There are other noble and necessary elements in the true Protestant faith, at which we can only hint. Protestantism has always been interested in *spiritual experience,* and therefore in living and vital religion. It is essentially a religion of the present and future. It venerates the sacred past and believes in it; but chiefly as a means of serving present needs and future opportunities. Protestantism is the living religion of the Living God. There is no tradition of the past which it holds more sacred than the present spiritual experience of living believers. It says to every man what God said to Moses out of the bush, "The place whereon thou standest is holy ground."

It follows from this, as it should follow, that Protestantism is profoundly interested in present social outworkings of Christian faith and life. It is significant that wherever Protestantism has gone, especially in its Reformed or Calvinistic form, it has instinctively allied itself with popular movements, with struggles for democracy and human freedom and enlightenment. It was the faith of William the Silent in Holland, of Cromwell in England, of the men who, at King's Mountain, broke the back of British tyranny on this continent. Calvinists have been famous, at times notorious, for their social and political activities. They have viewed their religion as a power to be set to work and made effective in all human affairs.

Protestantism, at its best, when true to its real spirit and genius, has ever been unafraid in the presence of facts, new or old: it has been the religion of the open mind, of the honest conscience, of the daring spirit, of the pioneer in truth and action. It has been and is, in truth, a broad, liberal, comprehensive faith, grounded in the firm acceptance of Christ and His Gospel, and committed to the open and free way of every soul to the finding of God, truth, and duty.

That is the sort of faith that drove these exiles across the sea three hundred years ago. That is the sort of faith needed to-day. There are certain facts which show with crystal clearness the indispensable value and necessity of such a Christian faith just now.

It is becoming more and more clear that the world needs and must have a universal religion, to serve as a unifying force among men. Romanism cannot meet this need. Only a religion at once strong and elastic can win and serve all the world of mankind. No religion calling for blind submission to external authority can possibly appeal to the world of this

day. Nor can any one variety of religious experience
and practice. The day has gone by for expecting
that all men will some time be Presbyterians or Bap-
tists; or even that they will all some day accept the
creeds and traditions of sixteenth century Reformers.
Only a moving religion, a religion that can go ahead
without losing touch with the past, can have the
slightest hope of being a religion for all the world.
And that means a religion of the spirit, such as Protestantism is at heart: a religion content to hold up
Christ, and to let Him say to all men, "I am the way,
and the truth, and the life," and to trust all men,
and urge all men, to find for themselves that way,
that truth, that life; a religion generous, comprehensive, large-minded; finding a sufficient unity in devotion to the personality of Christ and to His cause,
with large liberty of definition and interpretation.

The world is lost religiously unless it can be shown
a religion able to grapple successfully with modern
science and with modern industry, and to fill them
with the right spirit. Christianity is the only religion that has made the slightest attempt to fit itself
to modern science and to modern industrial conditions; and it is Christianity in its Protestant form
that has done this with real seriousness. It has not
done it wholeheartedly as yet, nor without serious
and violent opposition, both from within and from

without its own ranks. But nowhere in the world is there any religious body that is even making an effort to meet the modern world honestly and master it for God, except in the Protestant Churches. If that is not a call to Protestantism for a new depth and height of loyalty, what could be? The world is waiting for just such a religion as we might provide, were we in earnest. Dare we do less than our utmost?

Protestantism alone, the religion of the free soul, of the open mind, of joy in truth, and trust in the Bible as the revelation of God in terms of spiritual experience, Protestantism alone can meet the religious needs of the great and growing body of students in our country. It is a mighty and significant phenomenon, comparable to some of those great instinctive mass movements to which we look back in history with interest, this rush of eager youth that overflows and embarrasses all our educational institutions. More than ever before in any land, the student body, the educated folk, must be reckoned with here in America. The only religion that can appeal to them and hold them is a truly, vitally Protestant Christianity. Either they will wander with only a vague and passionless belief, or they will live in compartments, their religion shut off from their intellectual and practical interests, unless we can give them a true religion of the spirit, centered in Christ, Christ freely offered, Christ freely interpreted, Christ the Lord of their life and of the world's life, a religion that leaves ample play for the free intellect, for the free conscience, for forward movement. Only true Protestantism has such a faith to offer.

There is a vast mass of folk outside the churches, or but loosely affiliated with them, who must be won and held, if the church of Christ is to play its right and full part in the life of this country and this period. Here also there is no hope in religions of authority. These thoughtful masses—more thoughtful than often we imagine—cannot be driven or scared or coaxed into the church. They can be won only by a faith and spirit not afraid to come out into the open, to meet honest questions with honest dealing and without dogmatism, to set its Christ, its Bible, and everything it has and is, where all men can see and handle and judge for themselves. A religion with anything to hide is already discredited. A faith that must continually beat about the bush will not get far.

To one who views the conditions of to-day with open eyes and honest mind, there comes a tremendous call for a revival of *true* Protestantism; not the Fundamentalism that walks backward with its eyes on the past: not the Modernism that rushes forward,

William P. Merrill, D.D.

careless whether it keeps the path; but true Protestantism, the religion of the free soul and the open Bible, the religion of the spirit, the religion that is bold and broad and ever moving on, and that trusts ultimately and unreservedly in that Spirit of the Living God who speaks in the Bible, and lives and works unceasingly in the soul of man.

Not Protestantism as a negative, critical, vague, cool attitude of soul: not what Protestantism too often is, an indifferentism, an intellectualism, on the one hand content with the mechanical holding of certain doctrines, on the other proud of the freedom which means lack of conviction: that sort of Protestantism is not what we need. We have too much of it. That which we need, that for which we ought to be on our knees crying out to God in prayer, that which ought to be like a fire in our hearts and minds and bones, is the faith of the ancient prophets, the spiritual grace of the Lord Jesus and His apostles, the strong passionate conviction that God is here with us now, and that all our hope is in Him, that we know Him in Jesus Christ and in this rich, wonderful Word of His; and that the only way by which the world can be saved is by having Christ and the Word of God freely set in the midst, for every man and every group of men to lay hold of as they will, in the light of their honest convictions.

The True Protestantism

Not a *protesting* religion, in the ordinary, narrow sense of that word; a religion on the defensive, in the opposition; but a *Protestant religion*, bearing witness *for* the great, eternal truths by which men live, not afraid to give its testimony in the open, and to stand by it—that is the religion that is needed to-day. It is our splendid privilege to set it before men in winsome and compelling form.

"The just shall live by his faith." This is the age-long motto of the religion of free souls. But we need to take it in a new sense, which yet shall be its original sense. For it means most of all that faith is that by which true men *live;* and that the test of the reality of one's religion, the ultimate, decisive test, is not what he thinks, or what opinions he holds, but whether he *lives by* the faith he professes. Too many of us are negative Protestants, defending our freedom from priestcraft, and superstition, and ecclesiastical tyranny, and forms and ceremonies, priding ourselves on our liberty, but content with a lazy liberty. Oh, for a passionate Protestantism, not fanatical, free as God's air or sunlight, but as wholly devoted to God and to His free truth as was the Master himself, fervent in devotion to our free heritage. I call you and myself to a new loyalty, a new commitment to the true religion of the spirit, that we shall be indeed "Protestants"—witnesses to the faith in which we believe, loyal, devoted, unwavering in our service of the free religion of the spirit and of the Word; fulfilling the noble ideal set in glowing words by a great Protestant leader:

"To live by trust in God; to do and say the right because it is lovely; to dare to gaze on the splendor of naked truth, without putting a false veil before it to terrify children and old women by mystery and vagueness; to live by love and not by fear: that is the life of a true brave man, who will take Christ and His mind for the truth, instead of the clamor of either the worldly world or the religious world."

God help us to heed the call that comes to us to-day from a world in need of a saving of faith, and from a Christ waiting to save!

THE ULTIMATE GROUND OF HOPE

Last April the Old South Church of Boston observed the fortieth anniversary of the installation of Dr. Gordon as its pastor: a happy and historic occasion celebrating a memorable ministry. It was a day of joy not only for a great Church, but for a vast host of young men who owe the gracious preacher an unpayable debt, both for personal friendship and spiritual guidance. A Scotsman born in 1853, Dr. Gordon took his theological training at Bangor Seminary, afterwards graduating from Harvard University; and having served his apprenticeship in two village pastorates, he came to Old South Church in 1884. Besides making his pulpit a throne of power, as overseer of Harvard University, as lecturer on the Ingersoll, Lowell, Beecher, and Taylor Foundations, as well as in his books, he has been a preacher-theologian, a philosopher with the vision of a poet, a vital and constructive thinker in an era of theological confusion: as I have described him elsewhere, "a preacher whose sermons are lyrics and whose theology is an epic." If one were asked to name the two volumes of Best Sermons in our time, some of us would select *Through Man to God* and *Revelation and the Ideal:* the first a theodicy of amazing beauty and splendor; the second a series of visions in which the grand ideality of religious faith, shining through the cathedral windows of Bible literature, casts its revealing light upon the issues of character and the awful tides of human circumstance. There is about the man, as he fares toward sunset, a grace of character, a wisdom of faith, an old-gold mellowness of soul, and what Carlyle felt in Chalmers, "a serenity as of the on-coming evening and the star-crowned night." Who can better set forth the ultimate ground of that Eternal Hope by which the pilgrim generations of humanity have been lighted, lifted, and led?

THE ULTIMATE GROUND OF HOPE

GEORGE A. GORDON, D.D.

OLD SOUTH CHURCH, BOSTON

"Now the God of hope fill you with all joy and peace in believing, that ye may abound in hope, and in the power of the Holy Spirit." Romans 15: 13.

Our life has three dimensions: the past, the present, and the future. And our God answers to our life as thus defined, the God who was and who is and who is to come. The believing soul receives help from the Infinite One through memory, through experience, and through hope. Christian history, Christian experience, and Christian hope, these are the channels along which the consoling and creative might of God comes. The Christian soul is a king with an army: memory is the rear guard, the center is experience, and the vanguard hope.

There are many sources of hope. There is temperament; some human beings are so constituted that the darker the day, the muddier the road, and the more distressing the circumstances of the pilgrimage, the heartier, the wittier, the brighter, the more hopeful they become. What an amazing gift such a temperament is, what a boon such a soul, singing like the bird in the black shadow of the gathering thunder-storm. Other men are hopeful because they are in the prime of life. Again, if they are worthy of their superb physical existence, they are a vast blessing to their fellowmen. You have seen them, men so strong, so healthy, so vital, that they cannot imagine why anybody should not hope. There are others hopeful because of easy circumstances in life; others because they have a great capacity for friendship, which has been fortunately met. We are all more or less hopeful because we are citizens in a young, mighty, and growing nation. Others are hopeful because they are succeeding in their various occupations and professions; success creates hope. And others still, nobler perhaps than any I have already mentioned, are full of hope because they share in the best enterprises of their time.

I mention these sources of hope not to discuss them, but on the way to the great, ultimate ground of all hope, that is, God and the character of God. There is but one reason for hopelessness in our life, only one. If there is no God at the head of the Universe, if there is no Ruler of men and of nations, if there is no Heavenly Father, if the Universe has no heart of fire and soul of pity for man, if there is no Intelligence and Goodwill in command of the whole business of being, then hope is an illusion; a ship at sea without a navigator is a hopeless ship.

I remember passing once an abandoned ship in mid-ocean. Our great steamer swung out of its course and round the poor, doomed craft, to see if anybody alive was on it. It was sunk almost to the water's edge, tossed to and fro, the waves breaking over it, the canvas torn into ribbons; it was doomed; it was a melancholy and an unforgetable spectacle. But such would be our Universe by itself, unnavigated, unguided, uncontrolled, and unfilled with absolute Intelligence. There is but one fundamental, everlasting reason for hope; that is, God. If He is, then nature is but the expression of his Mind; in all its gloom and all its grandeur, it is still the shadow of God; all life is from his Life, all rational life from Reason in him, all moral life the breath of his Conscience; our human love and all the treasures of love are from Love in him. If we can repeat the Lord's Prayer, "Our Father, who art in Heaven, hallowed be Thy name, Thy Kingdom come, Thy Will be done in earth as it is in Heaven," and if that is our faith, then there is no room for anything but hope.

There are four classes of human beings for whom we may hope. First, those who suffer through ignorance, suffer terribly, suffer fatally. Think of the widespread suffering through ignorance; ignorance of physical law, ignorance of mental law, ignorance of moral law, and consequent torture of body, distress of mind, and woe of conscience. What a terrible world that is in which to live. And yet if there is a God in the world, we may hope for those who live there. We can see some ground for hope in their lives, and beyond there is God to take care of them where we are blind. In the first place, their suffering calls attention to the awful fact of ignorance. Ignorance is a wild beast, the worst wild beast in the world but one, perversity. A great cry of suffering comes from all parts of the world, and, in response, medical science, educational science, and religion come to the relief of the ignorant. And where we cannot see, God stands beyond. Surely, suffering does one thing, the suffering which comes through ignorance; it makes a man want to get out of it— and that is something—and out of that which leads to it.

There is the second class, those who suffer from the ignorance and from the brutality of others. Take the children of the world as an example; the children of a drunken father, the children of an ignorant and brutal mother, think of the woe in their life, and from those who have influence over them, from their ignorance and their wickedness.

The Ultimate Ground of Hope

The greatest example in all history of this kind of suffering is the Lord Jesus. He went to his cross on account of the ignorance and the wickedness of men; with what issue? The way of the cross is the way of light. In the tragedy of the life of Christ you are able to spell out a few meanings in the tragedy of the life of the world. He died on account of the ignorance and the brutality of his nation, and out of it has come the saving grace of the world. They who suffer from the ignorance and wickedness of others often and often become noble men and women, crying out to God for what they can get nowhere else, and through their suffering, let in light upon the general tragedy of the world.

The third class is the class of the wicked. Our fathers used to dispose of them very shortly—to Hell with them all when they die; after threescore years and ten, or any portion of that; if they were found on the wrong side, send them to their doom. That is no longer a belief among intelligent people in any part of Christendom. Why? Because the highest thing in the world, the Spirit of Christ, forbids it; because the highest thing in the Universe, the character of God, forbids it. We have hope for them. On what ground? Because, if you find yourself traveling against a storm, and that storm increases to a hurricane, and the road grows more and

more steep and dangerous, by and by you will find
that you cannot pursue that journey; you are on the
wrong trail. The stars in their courses fight against
the wicked man in his wickedness. The storm and
hurricane of God's government of the world blow in
the face of those who are walking the wrong way.
They may persevere, they may push on for a long
time, but no man can win against God. That does
not mean that scoundrels, blackguards, thieves, cut-
throats, and murderers are to be carried to Heaven
on flowery beds of ease. It means simply that God
is reasoning with wicked men in the courses of their
nature and through their whole being, and that vital
argument will continue until they give in and quit
the business; and then they must travel back with
bare feet on the terrible road over which they have
come. The Universe is tender, but eternally just,
and no man can by a few tears wipe out a wicked
past, or by a few words of repentance adjust himself
to the stern conscience of the world. And all this is
grand, tragically grand. There is no fooling with
the Universe; we must pay our debts; but then God
will help us to pay our debts, however big they may
be, and therein is hope for the worst being in the
Universe.

In old Calvinistic Scotland, Burns wrote a poem
to the Devil, and he had the audacity, nearly one

hundred and forty years ago, to hope that Satan might be converted.

> Ye aiblins might—I dinna ken—
> Still hae a stake.

There is a chance for you yet. It is part of the longing of every noble soul for the redemption from wickedness, of every rational being, and it is part of the faith of the noblest soul that not even the Evil Spirit can win against the Almighty and good God.

The fourth class for whom we may hope is composed of our dead. We ask, how can they survive? Millions and billions of them have left the world; where are they? Their mental life was dependent upon their physical being, especially upon the nervous organism; when that was paralyzed in death, what became of their minds? And we pile up objections and doubts against faith in the continuance of the human spirit, all of these objections and doubts gathered from the limitations of our knowledge and the boundlessness of our ignorance. What is a cobweb in the path of a planet? And what are your difficulties and doubts to the Lord God Omnipotent if He wants to save your soul and keep it alive forever?

What is Christianity? It is the revelation of God as the Father of the world; the supreme significance

339

of Jesus Christ is this, his revelation of the moral being and fatherly love of God. "He that hath seen me hath seen the Father," and all the ages of Christian faith from the first have sustained themselves by the belief that the Infinite Mystery that we call God is as good, as tender, as merciful, and as mindful of man as Jesus Christ was in the days of his flesh. Remember that Christianity is our greatest religion, because it gives us the greatest rendering of the character of God.

Think, as we close, of the names for God in the New Testament: the Father of Lights, the Light in whom is no darkness at all, the Father of Mercies, the God of All Comfort, the God of Pity, the God of Peace, the God of Patience. This poor, confused, wild world is absolutely unable to exhaust His enduring compassion. He is the God of Love, and this morning the God of Hope.

If your child is sick, and your physician says there is good hope, that ends your fatal anxiety. If your boy has lived a bad life, and you are told that he has taken hold of the hope set before him and become a new man, peace comes to your poor heart. No man ever yet became a suicide who had hope.

Hope is one of the greatest things in the world. It is like the sun going ahead of our planet, blazing a path of light and glory for it. We cannot remain in the business of well-doing without hope, and we cannot remain seekers for the truth, for clearness, and for better views in faith, without hope. We cannot stand at the grave of our friends without hope. We cannot look out upon the tumult of the world in which we live, and the tragedy, without hope. Hope is absolutely indispensable to science, to philosophy, to government, to morals, to physical living, to the whole Universe. And for your faith there is the God of Hope.

Let us take this message home. We are made of flesh and blood; we have great capacities for suffering as well as for joy. We are traveling on our way; we have got to go on. How shall we go? With a great hope blazing a path for us through the night. Follow in the track of that hope. May the God of Hope fill you with all joy and peace in believing; may you abound in hope and live a life like the songbirds in the spring on the wing, with a lyric pouring from their heart every morning and every evening.

A SCRAP OF SUNSET

Dr. Huget is a native of Iowa, and began his career as a teacher, first in the public schools of the State, and later as Professor of Education in Coe College, and as University examiner and instructor in Education in the State University of Iowa. He left the university for the pulpit in 1903, has had fruitful pastorates at Cedar Rapids, Galesburg, Detroit, and since 1917 at the Tompkins Avenue Church, Brooklyn—one of the largest Congregational Churches in America. One of the best beloved men in the American pulpit, he unites the delicate insight of a poet with the practical capacity of a great pastor. With the exception of a little booklet entitled *What Would Lincoln Say to this Generation?* Dr. Huget has published little, and a volume of his sermons is long overdue. The sermon here included, weaving a text from an ancient Psalm with a line from Edgar Fawcett's poem, "To the Baltimore Oriole"—

"In some glad moment was it Nature's choice
To dower a scrap of sunset with a voice?"—

is typical of one aspect of a noble and gracious ministry; and it adds to the present volume the benediction of beauty.

A SCRAP OF SUNSET

JAMES PERCIVAL HUGET, D.D.

TOMPKINS AVENUE CONGREGATIONAL CHURCH, BROOKLYN

"In thy light we shall see light." Psalm 36: 9.
"To give the light of the knowledge of the glory of God in the face of Jesus Christ." 2 Cor. 4: 6.

For many years I have felt the peculiar beauty and power in the words of the Psalm, "In Thy light we shall see light." Yet, I have never used this text as a basis for a sermon. The sermon is there, and it is at once evident. It is one of the texts that have a message in the very wording and in the beauty of the thought. But, at the same time, I have never felt that I had fully caught the deeper inner meaning. Nor do I feel now that I have entered into all the treasury and significance and suggestion in these moving words. Yet a certain thought has been shaping itself for a long time in mind and heart, and because of certain reasons that thought has seemed now to reach the time for its wording.

One phase of this is quite familiar and often expressed. It is this: There is an understanding of the great spiritual message which comes to some men in special degree, by reason of the illumination of the spirit. This we call inspiration. And by this I mean that there is knowledge which men do not gain of themselves, knowledge which would be beyond their attainment, were it not that it is imparted, knowledge which comes to them, and through them to us, by way of God's revelation. We have also been accustomed to more or less closely associate and limit this conception of inspiration to its appearance in connection with the writing of the Holy Scriptures. We believe that these sacred writings contain the self-revelation of God. We believe that God has spoken thus for the instruction and guidance of men. We believe that holy men of old spoke as they were moved by the Holy Spirit.

Yet in all of this we have been too much accustomed to discuss the whole doctrine of inspiration as if it were quite apart from any such ordinary experience as our own. We have felt that that time was another time than ours; we have felt that the prophets belonged to another age and another experience; we have thought that God broke the eternal silence, but permitted that silence again to close in upon the life of the world. We have assumed that God spake to the fathers of old, but speaks thus to men no more. If this Doctrine of Experience is to be valid for us we must believe that the men

A Scrap of Sunset

of old who spoke as they were moved by the Holy
Spirit are in every sense our spiritual kinsmen. Does
it seem to be going beyond the truth of things to
recognize in our own highest moments, in the rare
but real hours when we see clearly, the presence of
some great truth and the same great revealing operation of the Divine Presence? The realm of the spirit
lies about us. It is as true for us and as near to us
as to our fathers. This is what Edwin Arnold means
in one of his profound and more elusive poems in
which he speaks of the "larger world upon our own
impinging," whereof we have swift glimpses and momentary glowing awareness. He compares this experience to our knowledge of "spacious circles luminous with mind," to the light which comes from the
hidden sun when some dark cloud is "touched to a
sudden glory round the edge." By this he would
mean that just as the ring of silver or gold, or rose
or crimson that borders the sunset cloud, is not
only in itself a thing of light, but that it is the revelation of the greater life of the unseen sun, so these
radiant and enlightened moments of the spirit are
the indications and proof of the eternal light-giving
spirit which thereby is made evident and knowable.

There should be something of the prophet in every
man. Every preacher, however humble, should have
some message of prophetic fire. Every Christian in

the pew should some time hear and some time re-
utter the voice of the Spirit. Yes, there should be
something of the prophet in every man. He should
have awareness, however partial; he should have beholding, however dim; he should have knowledge,
however incomplete, of reality beyond his immediate
experience. God speaks to every man who will hear.
Certainly we have no warrant for supposing that the
Holy Spirit becomes silent. We remember Lowell's
great assertion that "God is not dumb, that He should
speak no more."

I have called this sermon "A Scrap of Sunset."
The phrase is borrowed from a poem by Edgar Fawcett in which, writing of the oriole, he speaks of the
glad moment when it was Nature's choice to "dower
a scrap of sunset with a voice." Yet, what should
this scrap of sunset or any other fragment of glory
be but the immediate reflection of a vaster beauty,
a more perfect splendor? The sunset itself, all of
it, is but the cloud-reflected light from a hidden sun.
And our high moments are times when we have some
glimpse of the wonder and beauty of God's world.
And thus, therefore, it is that these scraps of sunset,
these moments of vision revealed and declared, show
us that there is a surrounding universe of light and
truth and beauty. And it is from these first glimpses
that men reach on to their fuller knowledge. It is

from these prophetic splendors that men, by the eye and faith, behold the invisible.

Think for a moment how this is true in the great truths of science. They have always been true. Men have ever lived in a universe of order and of law. But men have not always known these truths. One day some man got the first thought of it—caught the first glimpse of it. Imagine the gropings of daring thought in the mind of the savage as he wonders about the flow of the rivers and the shining stars; imagine the world-changing moments when a Copernicus or a Columbus first compasses in fearless thought the idea of a new universe or of continents beyond uncharted seas; imagine the world-changing moment when a Newton lays hold upon the idea of universal gravitation, or when an Edison or an Alexander Bell first realizes that light or sound may travel along a wire. Somebody thought it first. Everything which we have gained in the world of knowledge was one time new. Way back yonder some one thought that a stick over a stone could be used as a lever to lift heavy weights, or that a log could be used for crossing the river to the more desirable hunting ground on the other side; or that sparks from chipped flint might kindle a fire for the warming of his fingers or the cooking of his food; somebody thought that wheels might be used, that a fiber of the palm might be woven into cloth for garments or for sails which the wind might fill, to drive the first ships. Somebody thought that signs might be scratched on the rock; that movable letters might be used for the printing of books; that steam could be harnessed for the driving of engines; that healing properties of plants might be used; that anesthetics may be utilized to deaden pain. Somebody thought it that sounds have meaning, and that was speech; that sounds have rhythm, and that was poetry; that sounds may be in tune, and that was music. Somebody thought it that men might gather together in groups, and that was the tribe; that there might be agreement as to customs and traditions, and that was government and law; that there is power in ourselves that works for righteousness, and that was faith and prayer.

In this realm of religion, not less than elsewhere, there have been men of spiritual genius, who first thought thoughts of God in the kingdom of the spirit. How sublime a poem the First Chapter of Genesis! How noble an utterance the Ninetieth Psalm! How ageless the beauty of the Song of the Shepherd! Each of these great utterances of the spirit, beautiful in itself, is as a scrap of sunset, revealing the greater glory of the other shining light which truly giveth light to every man.

A Scrap of Sunset

Now, any man whose eyes are not darkened may behold the sunset, and any man whose spirit is not clouded may have some glimpse of prophetic insight. There come to many of us moments of genius when we feel deeply and truly, when we see clearly and see far. And there come to all of us our times of at least some measure of understanding of the things of the soul. Why then can we not believe in our highest hours? Why can we not trust in our flashes of insight when we see above and beyond our ordinary vision?

The Christian should see things, not in seeking for signs and wonders, but by the light of a true spiritual understanding. He should see the common things more clearly, and see their meaning and their beauty. He should be prophet and poet. He should be able to see the oriole as a scrap of sunset and the sunset itself as the gleaming of a universal beauty. And above everything else, he should see the great things. He should see the goodness and the glory of God. He should see the meaning and value of His Kingdom. He should see Jesus as the fullness of the Father's glory, as the revealer of the Father's love. "He that hath seen me hath seen the Father." It is in this sense particularly and greatly that every Christian should be a prophet. Not the prophet of a magical foretelling or of a mystical pretense, but

351

the prophet of a clear beholding, of a deep understanding and of a blessed imparting to his fellows of that which his eyes have seen and his ears have heard of the mysteries of God, that thus to him and to his fellow man may be given to receive the fulfilling of that promise that he should be given the light of the knowledge of the glory of God in the face of Jesus Christ.